ADVANCE PRAISE FOR IT IS WELL

"The American Church is in a divine moment where Her auxiliary self-definitions are being shaken and most importantly Her core DNA is being re-discovered. The Church is being forced to find Her biblical identity and chief among these definitions is to be a family of generational faith transfer among all ethnic groups. While many churches may espouse this value, few have the tools, understanding, or the perspective to deal with the growing generational gap taking place in their sanctuaries, youth rooms, and nurseries.

In her book, Kayleon Dortch-Elliott provides a historical, sociological, and spiritual journey that will give any church leader a map to begin the much-needed work of bringing Abraham, Isaac, and Jacob to the same table to eat together at the same time."

Joel Solomon, Pastor and Professor
New Life Church and Regent University

"At a time when the wells of God's people are empty and broken, Kayleon Dortch-Elliott prophetically calls forth the Abraham, Isaac, and Jacob generations to re-dig them. She writes with prophetic insight and unusual clarity concerning the current state of the church juxtaposed with the biblical mandate to nurture intergenerational faith.

Her book is a must-read for all generations—especially Millennials—to reclaim the spiritual wells dug by their forbears. Her message is clear: come to the well that never runs dry."

Diane J. Chandler, Ph.D.
Associate Professor of Christian Formation
and Leadership, Regent University
Author of Christian Spiritual Formation: An Integrated Approach
to Personal and Relational Wholeness

"In *It is Well*, Kayleon Dortch-Elliott offers a compelling comparison between Abraham, Isaac, and Jacob's faith journeys and the spiritual experiences of recent generations, especially the Baby Boomers, Gen Xers, and Millennials. Her insight into the experiences of each generation is profound, and how stories from the biblical patriarchs apply to the present situation is impressive.

Throughout the book, Dortch-Elliott masterfully uses spiritual analogies and metaphors, urging readers to cherish the wisdom of the past while forging new paths for the future. Her book will encourage younger generations looking for a biblical way to understand the struggles of intergenerational dynamics."

Dr. Jeff Gossmann
Director of Campus Ministries, Regent University

"This book is a beautiful depiction of our need as Christ's followers to acknowledge and be grounded in our roots of faith, while simultaneously being open to how the Lord will guide us in new ways. Amazing connections and insights between the Patriarchs and the generations of our time will encourage you, deepen your appreciation for those who have gone before, and inspire you to leave a legacy of faith for future generations."

Adrianna Card
Former Overseas Missionary
Wife and Mother
Relations Lead at Messenger International

"*It is Well* is a thought-provoking book which delves into the complexity of generational faith. It offers liberation to Millennials who feel bound by tradition and find themselves questioning what their faith should look like in this ever-changing world.

Kayleon beautifully weaves generational patterns and issues of faith with well-known Bible stories we all grew up reading, encouraging each reader to embrace a personal relationship with God. A must-read for parents wanting to understand how they and their family fit into God's master plan, and the impact their faith has on their legacy."

Kashina Smith
Preparing the Home

"*It Is Well* underscores the profound connection between His word, our decisions, and the spiritual legacies we forge. Kayleon Dortch-Elliott delivers a compelling message to prioritize God's kingdom in our faith journey, marking an essential read for anyone eager to cultivate and craft meaningful faith that spans generations to come."

Jordan P. Barnes, Author, One Hit Away: A Memoir of Recovery

"What a thrill to read Kayleon's authentic and biblical-ly-guided interpretation of God's great love and comfort for us over the generations. Her book will undoubtedly prove to be a crucial tool for today's followers of Jesus as we all navigate cultural draws away from God's truth. She instead offers a wealth of vitally important reminders of divine grace, peace, and everlasting promises to cling to as we go about Kingdom work one day at a time. So thankful for her unmistakable gift to the world through these pages!"

Kyle Renee Moss, Executive Director of Impact,
Joyful Mindset Coach, and Author of Awaken Your Joy

It is Well

Generational Faith That Never Runs
Dry

Kayleon Dortch-Elliott

Contents

To my children.

Before I became your mother, I was afraid you wouldn't be ready for the world in the state it's in. But the more you grow, the more I realize the world isn't ready for *you*.

You are a gift to your generation.

And though you may follow in my footsteps for a while, I hope you'll dare to go a step further when it's time.

Foreword

I am a Baby Boomer.

Visions of sugar plums are not prancing around my head, and I can almost guarantee you that the Gen Xers and Millennials could not boast of this beatitude. Why? Because we are living in chaotic, uncertain, and perilous times. Times fraught with widespread corruption, injustice, racial bigotry, death, and fear. Adding to the above woes is a blatant disregard for the sanctity of life—prompting one to echo the words of the prophet Ezekiel: "The land is full of bloody crimes and the city full of violence" (Ezek. 7:23).

Kayleon Dortch-Elliott is well-versed with the current spirit of the times. In her book, *It is Well: Generational Faith That Never Runs Dry*, she offers valuable insights into tackling faith-related issues and spiritual aridity, which are plaguing the lives of so many today.

Drawing on the symbolism of wells, with their historical significance and diverse functions, she posits that *faith* is also a well. However, while it can be a valuable source of spiritual fulfillment, many have found it difficult to draw from in a way that meets their spiritual needs.

She goes on further to say that faith is intergenerational and that God has an intergenerational plan. In a novel and imaginatively clever manner, the writer parallels the lives and faith of Abraham, Isaac, and Jacob, with that of the Baby Boomer, X, and Millennial generations. She maintains that like these renown patriarchs, each generation must be true to the generational challenges of their day while also honoring the steps that have brought them to their present places.

This thought-provoking and timely book is a reminder that no matter what generation we belong to, God is still in control! And that we all have a part to play in carrying out His universal plan of salvation.

It is a call to the righteous to fortify their wells of faith, making certain that no leakages are present. For the weary of heart and all they who hunger and thirst after righteousness, the writer exhorts the spiritual seeker to follow the Lord Jesus' admonition in Mark 11:22: "Have faith in God" (NIV).

"[For] the LORD's hand is not shortened, that it cannot save, or his ear dull, that it cannot hear..." – Isaiah 59:1 (ESV)

Ron Dortch

It is Well
Poem Written by Ashley Moyo

On days,
the baton of faith is heavy to carry
and you find your faith
nothing but a ruptured bucket
drawing from your well
becomes an everlasting thirst
Water that is not living will never quench thirst
For without living water
What is well, but the absence of God?
What is well, but an inheritance
begging to be filled?
What is well, but place for burial?

So on those days,
remember

The baton of faith is an heirloom of Abraham
Within your palms, seeds of abundance
An authority to live in places beyond
and to take dominion
Carving paths for those to come
Many may come to thieve the labour of your well
But they too will wither,
for source will not be present here

The baton of faith is an Isaac
An aisle, ushering flooded blessings
from the father to us
With the courage to step even further
begging to redig what was inherited
The baton of faith is always passed down

Today, the baton of faith is a Jacob
A well pointing towards the living water
For well that is living, is abundant
in the presence of God
Well that is living, is a self seeking of Christ,
Well that is living, is a place of revival

There are wells within that await
for you to call upon them
Wells that know you by name
Don't shy away to dwell in Him
for it is always Well

It is Well

Generational Faith That Never Runs Dry

by Kayleon Dortch-Elliott

"Our descendants will serve him. Those who are not yet born will be told about him. Each generation will tell their children about the good things the Lord has done."
- Psalm 22:30-31 (ERV)

Introduction
Generational Wells

W ater wells have existed for nearly 8,000 years. The first well that was discovered is believed to have been dug during the Neolithic Era, around 7,000-10,000 B.C. In Ancient Mesopotamia, the patriarchs, Abraham, Isaac, and Jacob, dug wells with the help of their servants and mules.

Digging wells necessitated extensive manual labor, co-operation, dedication, and patience. There was more to it than simply digging and filling. Functionality was also part of the equation. As wells got deeper, the risk of cave-ins increased. As a result, the diggers had to collect sturdy material to line the walls. Shallow dug wells were prone to contamination, while deep ones were difficult to draw from. Digging a well was not an overnight project. Depending on how deep the well was and how many people were digging, digging a well could take several months.

In biblical times, wells served economic, social, and spiritual purposes. First, wells supported livelihood. Because of the unpredictability and lack of rain in the Middle East, people relied on wells as primary sources of water for themselves and their animals. They built them inside and outside of cities (Gen. 24), near encampments, and even in the desert (2 Chr. 26).

Second, wells were landmarks dug with the purpose of marking pivotal points along the journey. Naming places such as wells after divine encounters or significant events was common practice in Scripture (Gen. 16).

Third, wells were a symbol of status. They were claims of ownership or possession of the land or territory in which they were located (Gen. 26). With this, they served as practical inheritance passed down throughout generations.

Fourth and finally, they were symbols of community. Because wells represented supply and provision, people considered a community a thriving one if it had functioning wells. Wells were places of agreement and meetings for local citizens, frequented by women and travelers.

The mention of wells, pits, springs, and cisterns in Scripture carries significance, both literally and figuratively. It is remarkable how one seemingly simple structure can serve so many purposes within society.

In Protestant faith in America, wells carry a two-fold meaning. They represent intergenerational faith and individuals' inner lives. Abraham, Isaac, and Jacob, the patriarchs of faith, dug and re-dug wells that were passed down as inheritance throughout their lifetimes.

In those days, people depended on wells for water to live and work. In ancient times, they drew water from wells with buckets for various purposes throughout the city. Digging wells was not exclusive to them, however. The water extracted from our souls assists us today in interpreting the world around us.

God's mandate since the Old Testament is for every generation to familiarize their children with Him, give testimony of their own experiences with Him, instruct them on His principles, and admonish them to have reverential fear and devotion exclusively towards Him.

Throughout this book, I will parallel the lives and legacies of Abraham, Isaac, and Jacob with those of the Baby Boomers, Gen Xers, and Millennials. Each generation's exploration of faith uncovers themes that impact faith spiritually, socially, and economically. These themes have served as buckets for them to draw water from their inner wells. We will explore how the wells passed down and inherited by these three generations influence our approach, understanding, and reasoning of faith today.

IS IT WELL?

Two tasks associated with intergenerational faith have turned out to be more complicated than we thought. One involves respecting the tradition of faith, while the other involves grasping the significance of God and faith in the context of our own generations. It has been especially difficult given the shift of religious boundaries between each generation. These shifts stem from our frustration with ancient wells that appear to be no longer functional in our modern contexts. As a result, some have avoided the Christian faith or abandoned it altogether. Others have embraced the wells of faith passed down to them from preceding generations.

In each generation's effort to comprehend God's relevance and apply faith, there is a risk of creating broken wells (Jer. 2:13). Such wells are those we create for ourselves that cannot hold water. In our modern church culture, we are encouraged to dig wells that meet our personal criteria of right and wrong, our immediate needs, or what we think will benefit us most. Simplicity? A thing of the past. Standards? Too legalistic. The result is a prevalence of exclusivity, inauthenticity, superficial measures of spiritual growth, and divided affections.

The problem with broken, empty wells is less about the condition of the wells and more about how we've mastered the art of adorning them in their broken states. We acknowledge the existence of fractures in our faith and connections with God, yet we've become skilled at disguising them. Our itineraries are full, but our wells are empty. We go through the motions because it's what we've learned, what we saw growing up, or what we've been told is appropriate for a Christian to do. But just as faith without works is dead, I would propose that works without faith are also dead. One can easily mistake religious subculture for evidence of kingdom living when simply going through the motions.

Having faith in a Being that cannot be perceived through our physical senses is more challenging than we would like to acknowledge in altar calls or new believer's courses. Christ made it explicit to the disciples that following Him required putting others before oneself, sacrificing, enduring difficulties, and bearing a cross. The unappealing nature of the invitation did not stop the disciples from leaving their routines, careers, and homes immediately to follow Him. In many of our local churches today, we are hesitant to share the gospel in its truest and purest form. We tend to dress it up, giving more importance to our delivery than to the gospel itself.

Consider the car salesperson who cares more about what's in it for him, beating the competition, and how the sale will make him look to the rest of his team. Many Christians have magnified and highlighted the most marketable aspects of the gospel while relegating the less attractive truths to the fine print.

We rarely discuss how Christians are not immune to mental health issues, addictions, divorce, terminal illnesses, war, and injustice. We fear that conversations surrounding sacrifice and suffering will run people away. Thus, we market the gospel of salvation as a customizable remedy with promises of ready-made answers and benefits rather than an intimate bond with Christ.

This has done more harm than intended. It has surprised some Christians to find that Christian living is not as magical as it appeared to be. When the narrative used to evangelize them conflicts with their actual life, they become uncertain of how to navigate the complexities of faith. They default to questioning their identity and/or God's existence because they have not delved into a deeper understanding of either beyond a satisfying Christianity. They are uncertain where to voice their questions without facing rebuke for lacking faith in God, and how to reconcile with themselves for having questions in the first place.

As humans, we have spent centuries seeking to quench our thirst for belonging, love, and hope. Despite our efforts, nothing has been enough, and the gains we acquire only offer temporary fulfillment. Even our best attempts have left us unsatisfied. Our yearning is for a comprehensive spirituality, yet we seek wholeness in a fragmented world.

It is the functionality of wells that makes them so significant. A well dug without functioning capacity serves no purpose. Faith is deemed an indispensable well, but its function remains ambiguous. How relevant is faith to everything else I have going on? Where does God fit into the overall equation of my life?

To address this issue, we must accept that spirituality is not merely a component of our life. It *is* our life. When spirituality is only an aspect of our being, we can become overly rigid in its application and relevance to our lives. Second, we must remember that although God changes how He manifests or reveals Himself to different generations, *He* remains the same.

If we lose sight of these two principles, we may find ourselves promoting an a la carte faith, a Build-a-God culture, and DIY Christian journeys. If we are not careful to keep them at the forefront, a genuine relationship and life with God will become an option on a multiple-choice test. We will give in to the pressure to exchange the holy, faithful, loving, and jealous God for a passive, subjective god that satisfies our egos and whose identity conforms to our preferences.

We can find hope in that while we have our individual relationships with God and salvation to work out, faith is intergenerational. In this book, we will explore individual faith through the lens of God's intergenerational plan.

As you progress through this book, abandon the assumption that every question will be answered or issue resolved. As Paul wrote to the Corinthians, "our knowledge is partial and incomplete, and even the gift of prophecy reveals only part of the whole picture" (1 Cor. 13:9). No generation has a complete picture of the eternal God. However, our faith assists us in recognizing God during the current times and is not exclusively reserved for recognizing God in eternity.

Scripture tells us that the righteousness of God is revealed from faith to faith (Rom. 1:17). But what if transitioning from faith to faith was never meant to be a solo endeavor? Let this book be a reminder to you of the intergenerationality of God's eternal plan. When Christ returns, he is not coming back for one person alone, but for a Church—a collective Body. Our journeys are our responsibility, but don't forget to look around. You're not alone on this journey, and you never have been.

THE PAGES AHEAD

In part one, *Digging the Wells*, we will explore the lives and faith of Abraham and the Baby Boomer generation. Like

Abraham, each generation goes a step further than the previous generation. It's important for every generation to be adaptable to new ways of doing things while still recognizing and honoring the practices that have brought them to this point. We will explore pivotal events that molded the faith of the Baby Boomers, recognize their inner wells, and observe their encounters with God.

The second part, *Re-digging the Wells*, will have us seated alongside the well of Isaac's life and faith, as well as that of Generation X. Between the two widely known generations of Boomers and Millennials lies Generation X. Isaac finds himself sandwiched between Abraham, the father of many nations, and Jacob, the father whose sons became leaders of the twelve tribes of Israel. It might be easy to look over or to underestimate the significance of his story. However, Isaac's part in the fulfillment of God's generational plan and promise was no less significant than Abraham's and Jacob's. The same applies to Generation X. This generation faced famines like their parents but had different responses. They re-dug several of their parents' wells but also dug wells of their own.

In part three, *Moving Beyond the Wells*, we will begin by looking at Jacob's life story and his journey of faith in God. Jacob's journey and his wrestling with God were not for him, but for the tribes to come. Jacob's sons ended up becoming the leaders of twelve tribes of Israel.

The wells passed down to Abraham, Isaac, and Jacob served practical purposes, but we will delve into the spiritual significance that extended beyond the wells. The culmination of the former wells will be seen in Christ's interaction with the Samaritan woman at Jacob's well. Through Christ, the God of Abraham, Isaac, and Jacob reintroduced Himself as the living water that could quench all thirst.

The task of moving beyond the wells has been given to the Jacob generation, also known as Millennials. This endeavor involves a spiritual battle for Millennials as they attempt to pinpoint a reliable concrete structure for their faith. As with Jacob, Millennials are experiencing identity displacement and are wrestling with faith. We will explore the inner wells of the Millennials and draw attention to crucial events and cultural changes that have shaped and are shaping our faith. The final chapter will examine how to approach faith with future generations and tribes in mind.

··········

Generational faith is not the only inheritance. So is generational trauma. Given my background as a black woman raised in a black church, it is essential that I include in this book a discourse on the faith of blacks in America. For blacks, trauma is a solute in the water of our inner wells. As a society, we have made significant strides, but we are far from where we should be. Racism, injustices, and disparities have threatened to fracture our generational wells in the black community.

The question remains: How can brothers and sisters of all races walk together? By intentionally making room for the uncomfortable yet crucial truths of the black experience, we as a collective body will be better equipped to see God's will done on earth as it is in heaven, an inclusive will.

TO THE READERS

If you are feeling the weight of faith and questioning whether you are alone in this struggle, I want you to know that I wrote this book with you in mind. I pray this book serves you as Simon of Cyrene served Jesus by helping Him carry His cross; as the angel in Gethsemane ministered to Jesus when he prayed to have the cup of suffering taken away from Him; and as Aaron and Hur supported Moses' arms when he grew weary during battle. May this book help you bear your cross, minister to you before you give up on faith, and hold your arms steady during battle.

To the ministry leaders and groups seeking to explore intergenerational faith and reach multiple generations, this book is for you. The information contained in this book is neither all-inclusive nor all-exhaustive, but it is guaranteed to provoke conversation. I anticipate this book will be employed as a resource for a range of congregations, with the aim of gaining insight into the factors that have contributed to the faith of members from diverse backgrounds, age groups, ethnicities, and socioeconomic statuses. Additionally, I believe it will be a catalyst for holistic spirituality in local churches and a tool for more effective evangelism as you consider the inner wells of individuals you encounter.

Questions the Jacob generation may be asking about how their wells and Christianity intersect are ones I hope to answer. Questions like: *Where do we fit in the kingdom? How do we discern God's will for our lives? How is the Christian faith relevant to our contemporary context?* I hope you will bravely take on the responsibility of faith, which will directly affect the lives of your children and future generations. I hope you will handle your faith and the Christian life with caution, knowing that what you do now will outlive you. I hope you will build a life worth living for more than just yourself, and that you will approach generational wells with an eternal scope. May you have this book in hand when the pressures and temporal riches of this world lead you to forget what really counts.

My hope is that readers of every generation will gain a deeper appreciation for the faith of their ancestors and feel valued for the role they play in God's intergenerational plan. I pray you understand the significance of every step, the calculated ones and the missteps. We are saved by grace through faith, and it is *this* grace which has brought us thus far that will lead us home.

In Christ, your well and the generational wells to come will never run dry.

Truly, it is *well*.

Part I. Digging the Wells

Chapter One

ABRAHAM

Abraham is a patriarch in Christianity, Islam, and Judaism. In the Christian tradition, we recognize him as the "father of faith", revered for his unwavering faith and willful obedience to God.

He lived among polytheists who worshiped many gods. They did not worship these gods just for the sake of it. They worshipped the ones they believed could meet their diverse needs. For example, Baal was the god of rain, Anat was the goddess of war, and Astarte was the goddess of fertility. There were also deities whom they believed ruled over the sun and moon, sky and air, nature and harvest, sea, marriage, wisdom... and the list continues.

Some nations would physically carry their gods with them into battle, trusting that victory would come. These crafted deities lacked life, authority, and power, yet they were the objects of worship for the Canaanites. One, because humans who made crafted deities could manipulate, control, and destroy them if necessary. Two, because hundreds of gods sharing responsibility for order seemed more realistic than one God.

The false worship of the pagans emphasizes how miraculous it is that Abraham has become a patriarch of faith. His culture did not encourage worship of God alone, and his family members were also pagan idolaters and polytheists (Josh. 24:2), but God's call to Abraham changed the trajectory of his entire bloodline.

Abraham lived in his homeland of Ur for seventy years. After the death of Abraham's brother, their father, Terah, left their homeland and took the family with him to live in Canaan. The reason is not mentioned in the text, but on the way, Terah settled in the city of Haran and went no further. Terah died there and after five years in Haran, God instructed Abraham to leave—this time without his family. Abraham picked up where his father left off, but the call came at monumental risk.

To leave his homeland was to leave the comfort of a region he had called home for over 70 years. In his day, families represented security, stability, provision, safety, and significance. Families served as the primary source of connection for people, and they were commonly identified through their families. To leave his family, Abraham would abandon his cultural safety net. God was bringing him to a strange place, and he would have to start fresh and create his own identity with no one else's influence.

This must be why God said, "I will make a name for you." This was not about status and popularity. It was about having a secure identity in God. Can you imagine what it was like for Abraham having to start over in his seventies? How about the grief he experienced having to leave his family behind not long after burying his father? Though he willingly obeyed God's instructions, I imagine Abraham might have felt displaced. The weight of familial blessing was now on his shoulders, and it would be a long time before he saw the fruit of his obedience. But by faith, Abraham set out on an uncharted path. He left what was familiar on a promise from God and never looked back.

· · · ● ·● ·● ● · ·

Promises, or covenants, are thematic in Scripture, from the Adamic Covenant to the Messianic Covenant. Covenants were agreements between God and humans, outlining relationships and expectations. They provided structure, direction, and value.

In the covenant God made with Abraham, God promised land, descendants, blessing, and redemption. The Abrahamic covenant is unique in that it was an unconditional covenant. God promised to keep His word to Abraham and generations following, no matter what happened. Their behaviors and actions would not change God's mind about the end he destined for the descendants of Abraham. God was the only one expected to keep His part of the agreement. When later generations chose not to follow God's commands, God remembered His promise to Abraham and showed mercy.

· · · ● ·● ·● ● · ·

In Genesis 12, the first recorded famine is mentioned. It was severe, forcing Abraham to flee from Haran to Egypt for relief. While there, he deceived the officials by stating that Sarah was his sister rather than his wife. This was a half-truth, as Sarah was his half-sister. When the Pharaoh learned of Abraham's deception, he sent Abraham and all who were with him away. This would not be the last time Abraham would act deceitfully, and it would form a pattern for generations that were to come.

Although God had instructed Abraham to leave his family back in Haran, he decided to bring his nephew with him. After settling in Bethel, Abraham's herdsmen began disputing with his nephew Lot's herdsmen over the land. The land was not large enough to fit both Abraham and Lot with all their possessions. By the time they reached Bethel, Abraham's decision had come full circle. He learned that disobedience has consequences, even if it's only partial. Abraham and Lot ended up separating, and Abraham continued on with his wife and servants.

At 75, God promised Abraham that he and Sarah would give birth to a son in their old age. This came after Abraham revealed his worries to God about not having an heir. After the promise of a son, Sarah was still in disbelief, and she sought to convince Abraham to have the child of promise through her servant Hagar. Abraham gave in and had a son named Ishmael. As much as Abraham and Sarah desired to help God out, their solution was man-made, and Ishmael was not the son God had promised. God still promised to bless Ishmael because he was Abraham's descendant, but the covenant would remain unfulfilled until Abraham had a son with Sarah.

Twenty-five years after the promise, when Abraham was 100 years old, Sarah gave birth to a son named Isaac. Even a year's delay in the fulfillment of God's promise can discourage some of us. Imagine waiting 25 years and then being on the brink of losing the received promise not long after. When Isaac grew older, God tested Abraham by telling him to sacrifice his son on Mount Moriah. Right before Abraham followed through with it, the Lord miraculously provided a ram to be sacrificed in Isaac's place. Because of Abraham's obedience, God promised He would bless all the nations of the earth through his seed (Gen. 22:18).

DIGGING THE WELLS

When they came to Gerar, Abraham deceived Abimelech, the leader of the Philistines, just as he had done with Pharaoh back in Egypt. Eventually, Abimelech came to visit Abraham and wanted to make an agreement with him that they would treat each other fairly and truthfully. They formed the treaty at a well Abraham's servants had dug for him.

After forming the treaty, Abraham shared a grievance he had against Abimelech's servants for stealing his wells. This was the first Abimelech had heard about this. He did not recall Abraham complaining about it before. So, why now? Why was it important for Abraham to reclaim his wells? The Philistine leader thought it was a simple transaction, but it would have a long-term effect on Abraham and his descendants.

Abraham's wells, which were dug along his journey, acted as landmarks. They marked pivotal points throughout the journey. Abraham reclaimed ownership of his wells and named the one they were standing near Beersheba, meaning "well of the oath." This well of oath between Abraham and Abimelech would end up being the very place in which God would visit Isaac and renew the covenant he had made with Abraham. In claiming his wells, Abraham was pioneering faith for his family. These were not ordinary wells; they were generational wells.

THE GOD OF ABRAHAM

We are products of Abraham's faith—spiritual seed, heirs, and descendants. Abraham came to know God as the God of glory (Acts 7:2-3), the God of promise (Gen. 12), and the God who sees and provides (Gen. 22). This same God has revealed Himself to us.

We can learn from Abraham not to try assisting God with fulfilling His promises or with His provision for us. Abraham's mistakes occurred during moments when he felt most out of control or when there was a lot at stake. He lied to Pharaoh after fleeing to Egypt for relief from the famine because he feared for his life. He disregarded his doubts and had a son with Sarah's servant, because it did not seem like God's plan would work.

We can see the development of Abraham's faith, especially in his response to God's testing on Mount Moriah. His usual pattern was to take matters into his own hands when a crisis arose, yet he did not intervene to save himself or his son. When Isaac inquired about the lamb for burnt offering, Abraham said, "The Lord will provide Himself a sacrifice." We are not told whether his voice was shaking when he said this, or if he was too nervous to make eye contact with Isaac knowing what was to come. But we know that, confidently or not, Abraham trusted God and yielded to His control.

·····•·••··

I believe Abraham has become the father of faith, not because he got everything right, never erred, and always surrendered full control to God. He is a symbol of faith because his journey shows us the times when we are uncertain of God's work and the times when we search for the assuring presence of a God who doesn't seem to care about our lives.

We see the aftermath of Abraham's faith, but for him, it was moment by moment. We see how God providing the ram in Isaac's place foreshadowed God sending Jesus to take our place, but for Abraham, he trusted God when it made little sense. How was Abraham supposed to be the father of many nations and have descendants as many as the sand if his son was not alive to continue the lineage? When all the pieces were scattered, Abraham put his trust in God. We are testament that it was not in vain.

I often wonder how individuals in Hebrews, praised for their faith, would feel about or respond to the accolades we've given them. I imagine they might chuckle and say, *If only having faith was that simple. That only scratches the surface of my story.* Perhaps it would surprise them, and they would say, *I never expected this. I was only surviving.* Or maybe they would cry tears of joy and say, *Wow, everything I experienced really was worth it. What I considered mundane mattered.*

How redemptive it must be to see that the life you lived on earth became a source of inspiration for someone who never met you. I can imagine the great cloud of witnesses looking down on us now, jumping in anticipation and shouting from the top of their lungs: *It's all true! We were right about God all along! Just wait until you see Him! Just wait and you will see what it all was for! Please endure and don't abandon hope! Despite the difficulty, it pays off!* How resounding their "amens" must be to Paul's words:

> *"For our light and momentary troubles are achieving for us an eternal glory that far outweighs them all."*
> - 2 Cor. 4:17 (NIV)

> *"...what we suffer now is nothing compared to the glory he will reveal to us later."* - Rom. 8:18

The father of faith was no stranger to scarcity, struggle, or sacrifice. Abraham left the comforts of his homeland to become a sojourner. He was without the convenience of a house; he found shelter in tents in fields, deserts, and mountains. Like Abraham, the Baby Boomer generation did not grow up with the luxuries we have today. They made the most of what they had, and when they saw an opportunity to create what they had not seen, they took full advantage. We can learn from both Abraham and the Boomers to trust God's sufficiency, be a good steward, and sacrifice without knowing the outcome.

Boomer individuals dug wells that pioneered the faith of their children, grandchildren, and beyond. We will explore their faith journeys in the next chapter. Their obedience made a lasting imprint on their generation's faith, and we are reaping the harvest of it today.

Chapter Two

BOOMERS

P *erhaps the most influential generation in history.*[1] This is how Psychology Today refers to the Baby Boomer generation—individuals born between 1946 and 1964. For 20 years, over 4 million babies were born annually.

Baby Boomers followed the rules, emphasizing traditional structures in family, marriage, work, and society. Given the strength of the economy following World War II, Boomers became known for their 9-to-5 careers, record-high birth rates, ambition, and drive. While the Boomers had their share of good times in history, they were also subjected to the difficult-to-reconcile elements of the human experience, like any other generation.

They were front row center to major historical events, to include the Vietnam War, Civil Rights Movement, and Cuban Missile Crisis. As expected, the dissimilarities among individuals and groups pervaded the culture with enduring spiritual, social, and economic consequences.

Boomers wondered how God could be present in both peaceful times and in times of chaos, war, or division.

The Baby Boomer generation, just like Abraham, was given the responsibility of continuing the family name and heritage, as well as securing assets to be passed on to their children and grandchildren. Considering God's manifestation in future generations was not their top priority when they had their own spiritual paths to explore.

How did Boomer individuals deal with loss, pain, injustices, war, death, temptations, uncertainties, sin, and doubts? Regrettably, there was minimal inquiry about faith (at least openly), as many individuals were instructed that inquiring was equivalent to questioning God, which was viewed as blasphemous or indicative of disbelief.

Thus, Christians in this generation often prioritized faith over feelings. This resulted in an ambitious spirituality that was more about fear and duty than love and relationship. Boomer individuals adopted a legalistic approach in response to the human condition, similar to early Christians in the New Testament (Gal. 5:4-6). To obey was far more important to God than whatever you had to sacrifice to do so.

In the wake of the mid-twentieth century occurrences, Christian Baby Boomers found themselves serving a God they were afraid of, with God's principles being translated through the standards of the churches they belonged to. They prided themselves in what Christians in later generations view as "spiritual burnout." However, to them, it was their reasonable service and way of demonstrating their commitment to God and affection for each other.

Even now, this generation remains unrivaled in their giving, praying, serving, and church attendance. Local church attendance was used as a metric for determining a person's standing in society, particularly in the southern region of America. They understood church to be a primary source of a person's relationship with God rather than an extension of it.

Boomers were taught that God opens doors of opportunity daily, and that stepping out on faith requires sensitivity to God's leading. A major question of believers in this generation was: How do I know God is speaking? They wanted to know: What is important in life? Is what I'm striving for worth it? What is temporary and what is permanent? What is my purpose in life?

With time, the challenge for this generation of believers became apparent: acknowledging that their Christian faith has more to offer than a list of spiritual chores and guaranteeing a spot in heaven. They began to understand that the kingdom was more within reach than they once thought. An intimate relationship with God permits the present-day experience of His kingdom, and His intentions for our lives are not restricted to salvation. Christian Boomers came to desire experiences with God in their daily lives, as ordinary as they may have seemed. These newfound realizations challenged them to move beyond the facts of God to the experience of Him.

INNER WELLS

No generation has a complete picture of the eternal God. However, our faith helps us know God in the times we live in and is not just reserved for knowing God in eternity. With this in mind, I have surveyed literary works, sermons, and studies from each generation that I am convinced reflect the spirituality of the times.

E. M. Bounds, an author and clergyman from the 18th century, had most of his books published after he passed away. With a focus on prayer, his works responded to spiritual climates over several decades. A. W. Tozer, born in 1897, was not a Boomer, but also published works in response to the times.

Dallas Willard, born in 1935, was part of the Silent Generation. He published his first book when Boomers were between the ages of 20 and 38. He gained widespread recognition as a Christian philosopher and emerged as a key voice in spiritual formation. Richard Foster was born a few years shy of the Boomer generation and was another leading authority in spiritual formation.

Despite not belonging to the Boomer generation, these authors, among others, had a significant impact on the development of Boomers in their adult years. The fruit is shown in the work and ministry of Christian leaders born in the Boomer generation, including Max Lucado, Tony and Lois Evans, John and Lisa Bevere, Beth Moore, Tim Keller, John Ortberg, T. D. Jakes, John Piper, and more.

Abraham was not the only one who dug wells. Throughout church history, wells have represented our souls—our inner lives. In ancient times, people drew water from wells with buckets to serve various purposes throughout the city. Similarly, the water drawn from within our souls helps us interpret the world around us. Two revelatory themes have significantly influenced the spiritual, social, and economic dimensions of faith in the Boomer generation's exploration. These themes are buckets from which they drew water out of their inner wells.

DISCIPLINE

"Every age has its own characteristics. Right now, we are in an age of religious complexity. The simplicity which is in Christ is rarely found among us. In its stead are programs, methods, organizations, and a world of nervous activities which occupy time and attention but can never satisfy the longing of the heart. The shallowness of our inner experience, the hollowness of our worship, and that servile imitation of the world which marks our promotional methods all testify that we, in this day, know God only imperfectly, and the peace of God scarcely at all. If we would find God amid all the religious externals, we must first determine to find Him, and then proceed in the way of simplicity."[2] - A. W. Tozer

First is spiritual discipline. Richard Foster categorizes twelve main spiritual disciplines in his book *Celebration of Discipline* into three groups: Inward Discipline, Outward Discipline, and Corporate Discipline.[3] Inward discipline includes meditation, prayer, fasting, and study. Outward discipline includes simplicity, solitude, submission, and service. Corporate discipline includes confession, worship, guidance, and celebration. Three spiritual disciplines most frequently practiced by the Boomers include service, prayer, and simplicity.

The discipline of service is marked by purposeful, missional behavior that puts others first, and careful stewardship of the gifts given by God. Prayer involves ongoing communication with a God who is always listening and speaking. The practice of simplicity is about the reordering of one's priorities, the laying aside of every hindering weight (Heb. 12:1), and the distinguishing of temporary riches from eternal treasures (Matt. 6:19-20).

In 2007 and 2014, the Pew Research Center evaluated religious dedication amid diverse generational cohorts. They relied on self-reported frequencies of attending worship services and daily prayer, along with the individuals' conviction in God and the overall significance of religion in the individuals' lives. From both studies, an average of 61% of Boomers had a high level of religious commitment, 26% had a medium level, and 14% had a low level.[4]

Religiously, one could say that Boomers experienced an overemphasis on the outward disciplines. Their schedules were jam-packed, however, the call for spiritual self-control, or the reordering of their souls, would only allow them to engage in what was meaningful.

It was a call to accept the lighter load Christ offers in Matthew 11. The yoke He offers is still binding and requires effort, but we find the difference in grace. In *Renovation of the Heart*, Willard wrote: "The greatest saints are not those who need less grace, but those who consume the most grace, who indeed are most in need of grace—those who are saturated by grace in every dimension of their being. Grace to them is like breath."[5] Christ's invitation to an unforced, grace-filled rhythm is an invitation to no longer carry burdens alone.

Through the spiritual disciplines, Boomers were encouraged to partner with God in the kingdom's work instead of doing what they believed would "get them to heaven" or keep them away from the world and its pleasures. Rather than making assumptions about what might please or be acceptable to Him, they were invited to seek Him out to gain knowledge of His identity, likes, dislikes, desires, and specific purpose for their lives.

In an age of spiritual complexity, the beauty of simplicity was a treasure to be discovered. God said in Hosea 6:6: "I want you to show love, not offer sacrifices. I want you to know me more than I want burnt offerings." Similarly, His plea to the Boomers was: "I'm after love that lasts, not more religion. I want you to know God, not go to more prayer meetings" (MSG). To proceed in the way of simplicity required Boomers to slow down and consider who they were beneath all their doings. Spiritual disciplines prompted

Boomers to move beyond legalism and recognize God as both Savior and Lord.

EXPERIENCE

"For millions of Christians... God is no more real than He is to the non-Christian. They go through life trying to love an ideal and be loyal to a mere principle. Over against all this cloudy vagueness stands the clear scriptural doctrine that God can be known in personal experience."[6] - A. W. Tozer

The second theme which informed the faith of the Boomer generation is the experiential knowledge of God and His kingdom. This generation of believers is known for their no-nonsense approach, traditions, and unwavering loyalty to the local church. Christian Boomers prioritized conversion, church membership, and sainthood above discipleship. Many people only experienced God within the walls of their local churches.

In *The Pursuit of God*, Tozer describes the Christian faith during this time as characterized by "shallow lives, hollow religious philosophies, the preponderance of the element of fun in gospel meetings, the glorification of men, trust in religious externalities, quasi-religious fellowships, salesmanship methods, [and] the mistaking of dynamic personality for the power of the Spirit."[7]

Their faith was shaped by their experiences and the exhortation of church leaders, sometimes overriding Scripture. Mental illnesses were demonically influenced. Sickness was a job for God, not a physician. Spirit-led sermons trumped seminary-crafted ones. One mistake could leave you hell bound. Many preachers took scriptural passages out of context to advance diverse agendas. Some Christians elevated Scripture to the status of their Lord, surpassing God Himself, rather than using it as a means to an end.

The very faith proclaimed in corporate worship needed to be actualized in their homes, workplaces, and communities. However, fear acted as a barrier for people to gain greater knowledge about God and His kingdom during that period. Evangelism, sermons, and conversations often employed fear as a tool to underscore the significance of salvation.

Just as Boomers were thrust into adult responsibilities early on, many were also thrust into spiritual adulthood, without the chance to nurture a childlike faith. Children have an inherent curiosity and freedom to explore and ask questions, but it was frowned upon in their case. In fact, it was sinful, blasphemous even, to question God.

Spiritual leaders warned them as E. M. Bounds warned, "All questioning must be guarded against and avoided. Fear and doubt have no place in true praying."[8] Bounds was correct in his assessment of the necessity of faith and the impact that unbelief has on prayer's effectiveness. Throughout the New Testament, Jesus rebuked the disciples and others for their lack of faith, and he encouraged unwavering faith.

But where was the handbook on how to deal with times of uncertainty or doubt? How should we approach situations where belief and disbelief coexist, such as with the father in the book of Mark pleading for his son's healing (Mk. 9:24)?

Christians during this period did not openly discuss their questions, uncertainties, and doubts. Instead, they relied on interpretations of Scripture that offered healing, answers, and rewards, often without fully acknowledging the hardships that come with carrying one's cross.

One example is divorce. The U.S. Bureau of Labor Statistics conducted the National Longitudinal Survey of Youth, interviewing nearly 10,000 Boomers annually from 1979 to 1994 and biennially since 1994. The NLSY79 cohort included individuals born between 1957 and 1964 who were living in the United States when the survey began in 1979. For this cohort, the divorce rate was less than 50%.[9]

I'm interested in knowing if religious involvement in Christian faith contexts influenced how some individuals approached divorce during that period. Apart from this study, many Boomers from Christian backgrounds have expressed that divorce wasn't fully embraced in their faith communities.

Mental health is another reality. Mental illness was heavily stigmatized, along with other forms of disability. Boomers highly valued self-sufficiency, resulting in unaddressed mental illnesses. Even now, many Boomers disregard the importance of mental health treatment for their well-being and functioning.

On questioning, Dallas Willard wrote in *The Divine Conspiracy*: "The adult members of churches today rarely raise serious religious questions for fear of revealing their doubts or being thought of as strange. There is an implicit conspiracy of silence on religious matters in the churches."[10] Wavering in one's faith was a weakness, so they avoided questioning at all costs. Instead, they served more, gave more, quoted more Scripture, sang more songs, and attended more services. The more they did, and the faster the pace, the longer they could go without facing the questions their hearts longed answers for.

What appeared to be a display of great faith during adversity actually concealed feelings of anger, bitterness, distrust, lack of hope, and betrayal. The feelings are not unfortunate, but that they went unaddressed is. Willard wrote about this in his book, *Hearing God*: "Great faith, like great strength in general, is revealed by the ease of its workings. Most of what we think we see as the struggle *of* faith is really the struggle to act as *if* we had faith when in fact we do not."[11]

Did they have faith? Yes.

Did they *always* have faith? Not if they were human.

• • • ● • ● • • • •

Seeking a personal experience with God had major implications for this generation. In the 1960s, America underwent religious changes that would affect religion for the rest of the 20th century and on. The most notable movements of this generation occurred in the Religious Crisis of the 1960s.

Anglicanism saw the start of the Charismatic Movement, which then grew in mainline Protestant denominations. The Charismatics believed they had gained new insight into the Holy Spirit, miraculous manifestations, and the exercise of spiritual gifts. They believed that a relationship with both God the Father and Jesus was only complete with the Holy Spirit. They were passionate about seeing practical yet miraculous demonstrations of the Holy Spirit in their lives. This movement followed the Healing Revival and Latter Rain Movements that occurred between 1946 and 1958.

The 1960s to 1980s marked the period of religious television broadcasts, achieving a viewership of nearly 25 million people by the mid-1980s. Through these broadcasts, "televangelists" aimed to spread the gospel to more people and push back against radio platforms' restrictions on religious media airtime.

For many Boomers, radio and television broadcasts provided both spiritual encouragement and practical demonstrations of evangelism in their local areas. Certain televangelists capitalized on the Boomer generation's reverence for authority, often using faith through spiritual or financial manipulation to push their own agendas. As a result, some Boomers became distrustful of religious leaders and their representations of God.

The Boomer generation in America experienced other notable occurrences in addition to the Religious Crisis and the emergence of Christian television broadcasts. As Christianity became more diversified in its theology and practice, alternative belief systems were introduced and gained widespread acceptance in the nation.

A prominent movement which introduced an alternative system of belief was the New Age Movement started in the 1970s. The New Age philosophy had pantheistic, Gnostic, and esoteric origins. Instead of traditional spiritual disciplines, transcendental experiences and metaphysical healing were achieved through alternative practices, including tarot readings, yoga, astrology, mediumship, crystal use, and hallucinogenic drugs. According to New Agers, spiritual awareness and worldwide peace were the answers to humanity's problems, not God.

Before the 1960s, it was uncommon to be unaffiliated with Christianity or identify as non-religious. Prior to that, America was believed to be a Christian nation, given that a large portion of the population identified with a Christian denomination. Certain Boomers, as they sought to know God through experience and personal faith, continued to follow their faith traditions and religious duties from their upbringing. Others left their faith traditions to explore other beliefs or became unaffiliated with religion.

DIFFERENTIATED FAITH

The Boomer generation lived through the Segregation Period and the Civil Rights Movement. While discussing the faith of a generation that lived through these times, it's important to acknowledge that faith has taken on distinct forms and meanings for black Christians. When I look back on my upbringing, I recognize the importance of highlighting the role of faith and the church in the black community.

The faith of black Boomers has developed and taken on various forms throughout history. According to a study by the Pew Research Center on Black religious history in the United States, the majority did not practice Christianity before the 1700s. West African religions, Islam, and Catholicism were predominant religions among the enslaved population before they were taken to America.[12] Christianity was another pre-existing religion in Africa, and many Africans were believers. By the 1900s, many blacks had lost faith in both America and Christianity and turned to other religions.

· · · ● · · ● · · ·

The enslaved were forbidden from engaging in religious activities, like reading from the Bible, praying, or attending seminary. Slaveowners did this because they were scared the enslaved would see themselves as equals and rise up against them. They emphasized to the enslaved that accepting Christianity did not entitle them to freedom.

As a result, enslaved individuals who converted to Christianity resorted to secret meetings in slave cabins, the woods, or anywhere else they could without getting caught. Each time they met, they were putting their lives at risk, as slaveowners threatened to whip or flog them if they caught them.

Slaveowners hired and trained evangelists to preach to the enslaved as they were not allowed to read or receive any form of seminary education. Thus, enslaved Christians leaned on the Holy Spirit for revelation and divine knowledge in their secret meetings, as opposed to scriptural understanding.

Along with their secret meetings, certain enslaved individuals were occasionally permitted to attend white churches with their masters. Frederick Douglass spoke about the hypocrisy of his owner, who was also a class-teacher in a Methodist church. He spoke about the inner turmoil he experienced hearing his master's teachings and prayers, knowing he had just witnessed him whip his cousin.

On negro spirituals, Douglass wrote, "a keen observer might have detected in our repeated singing of 'O Canaan, sweet Canaan, I am bound for the land of Canaan', something more than a hope of reaching heaven. We meant to reach the north, and the north was our Canaan."[13] They certainly anticipated the kingdom of heaven. Still, there were more immediate hopes that would influence their life's journey, and therefore, freedom became their priority. Their spiritual meetings, though secret, gave them a sense of purpose, identity, hope, and meaning.

· · ● ● ● ● ● · · ·

Even after slavery ended, black people were not welcomed in white churches and, if they were allowed in, they had to stand in the doorway and were not permitted to take part in sacraments.

From the 1780s until the 1960s, black denominations, conferences, and movements emerged, allowing black people to worship without restrictions. The local church in the black community was a one-stop destination for hope, belonging, worship, education, business, leadership opportunities, social clubs, and economic relief.

The establishment of all-black churches was met with resistance, despite the romanticized view of newfound freedom in historical timelines. While blacks no longer had to meet in secret like their enslaved ancestors, many still worshiped in fear. Slaveowners were now embodied in black codes and white supremacist groups. The flogging and lynching of black bodies were now perpetuated in the burning and bombing of black churches.

Within a year of the bombing of 16th Street Baptist Church in 1963, 20 more black churches were bombed. As one might imagine, preaching hope was not a simple task. James Baldwin attests to this in *The Fire Next Time*, in response to the spiritual climate of the 1960s:

> *I was just as black as I had been the day that I was born. Therefore, when I faced a congregation, it began to take all the strength I had not to stammer, not to curse, not to tell them to throw away their Bibles and get off their knees and go home and organize, for example, a rent strike. When I watched all the children, their copper, brown, and beige faces staring up at me as I taught Sunday school, I felt that I was committing a crime in talking about the gentle Jesus, in telling them to reconcile themselves to their misery on earth in order to gain the crown of eternal life.*[14]

Understanding this history sheds light on why the local church, religious practices, and service attendance are important to black Christians of the Boomer generation. This context helps explain how black Christian Boomers could become legalistic, controlling, and overly obsessed with religious practices—the same practices they were once forbidden to partake in.

Moreover, it elaborates on the role of the local church in their spirituality and daily lives, the nature of sermons in black churches, and how Black Boomers learned to rely on God. It contextualizes the skepticism that many in the black community have had toward Christianity throughout American history. Black Boomers particularly held Christians responsible for carrying out religious obligations while disregarding the "weightier provisions", like justice (Matt. 23:23).

THE GOD OF THE BOOMERS

The wells Abraham dug were not only for him. They surpassed his lifetime and had a profound impact on the livelihood and faith of Isaac and Jacob's generations. Similarly, the inner wells of the Boomer generation and preceding generations have affected the faith of the generations that followed.

The faith of Boomers reminds us that to reign with Christ, we must share in His sufferings. Their faith teaches us that God's will extends beyond the four walls of the local church, and that a divided community cannot promote a unified faith.

Faith is handed down and cultivated from one generation to the next. In Part II, we will explore the wells of Isaac and Generation X. In the next chapter, we will discuss what happened to Abraham's wells, how Isaac re-dug the wells of his father, and how he went a step further to dig new wells of his own.

Part II. Re-digging the Wells

Chapter Three

ISAAC

I saac, the child of promise, was born to Abraham and Sarai in their old age. His name means "laughter" because Sarai laughed in disbelief at the possibility of having a child past childbearing years. Abraham and Sarai's patience was rewarded when Isaac, their long-awaited son, was born two decades after God's promise.

Once Isaac got older, God asked Abraham to sacrifice Isaac as a test of his obedience. The age of Isaac when it happened is uncertain, with some scholars estimating he was in his late teens and others suggesting he was in his twenties or thirties. The most important aspect is that God provided a substitute to replace Isaac before Abraham could carry out the act. Genesis 22 serves as a prefiguration of Christ as the only Son who, through His obedience, became our sin penalty substitute by His death.

In Genesis 24, Abraham instructed his servant to find a wife for Isaac. The servant prayed for guidance, and God directed him to Rebekah. He became her husband and fathered twin sons, Jacob and Esau.

According to Genesis 25, Isaac received a blessing and inherited everything that belonged to Abraham after his death. He adopted his father's profession as a farmer and herdsman, and through hard work, accumulated significant wealth in his adult years.

FAMILIAR FAMINES

It was common for Ancient Mesopotamia to face droughts and famines. In Genesis 12, right after God called Abraham, a famine of unprecedented proportions hit the land. In order to survive, Abraham had to leave and become a foreigner in Egypt. When he and his wife Sarai arrived, he decided not to reveal the complete truth about their relationship. He feared that the Egyptians would be mesmerized by her beauty, putting his life in danger.

This is an example of how famines lead to desperation. Abraham was prepared to do whatever it took to stay alive. So, to protect himself, Abraham fled to Egypt and used his wife (who was also his half-sister) to manipulate the Egyptians.

Isaac experienced famines just like his father Abraham did. Genesis 26 illustrates a pattern that spans generations, with a father and son exhibiting similar behaviors in times of crisis. It highlights the potency of generational patterns and God's awareness of our familial wiring.

In verse 2, "The Lord appeared to Isaac and said, 'Do not go down to Egypt, but do as I tell you.'" The interesting part about this is that the text never says that Isaac mentioned anything about going to Egypt. It is not out of the realm of possibility that the God who could understand the innermost thoughts of individuals in the New Testament (Matt. 12:25; Mark 2:8; Luke 6:8, 9:47; John 16:19), knew the heart and mind of Isaac. Isaac didn't need to explicitly state his plan to go to Egypt. Before Isaac reacted, God already knew what his immediate response would be.

God told Isaac to stick around where the famine was, and Isaac listened. However, just when it seemed like the worst part was behind him, Isaac repeated his father's mistake. Isaac committed a sin that he was predisposed to, even though he never saw his father do it. He mirrored his father's actions and falsely claimed that his wife, Rebekah, was his sister. He did as God commanded and stayed in Gerar but was still susceptible to repeating his father's mistake.

·· • • •· • • • ··

Isaac's famines were like his father's, but not completely the same. Different famines require different approaches, regardless of their familiarity. Isaac encountered spiritual obstacles both inherited from his father and individual to his own experience. The method Abraham used to approach obstacles before was no longer feasible, and God's covenant with Isaac was a clear indication of this. The instruction from God to Abraham was to depart and go, whereas Isaac was commanded to stay where he was. The family agreement was unaltered, but the way forward was distinct. The promise was consistent, but the plan varied. The covenant itself had undergone no changes, but it was the passage of time and the emergence of new generations that mandated a shift.

It is important to note that the words spoken by God in Genesis 26:3-5 were not simply a reiteration of the Abrahamic covenant. The establishment of God's covenant with Isaac was a way of ensuring the continuation of faith for the next generation. Isaac was not limited to the leftovers of Abraham's promise, nor was he living his life solely based on Abraham's relationship with God.

Although he was influenced by his father's faith, his own personal experiences would lead him to develop a special relationship with God that was entirely his own. As with his forefathers, Isaac was challenged to make changes and embrace a way of doing things differently than generations before.

RE-DIGGING THE WELLS

Famines represent loss. In the famine-stricken land, there was a looming possibility of starvation and death. Both they and their livestock faced the threat of starvation, malnourishment, and disease. Resources were limited. Food was allotted. Routines were interrupted. Choices were few and demand exceeded supply.

A famine was not a short-lived discomfort, but rather a prolonged ordeal that persisted for several years at a time.

The individuals who were affected had to deal with the difficult emotions associated with displacement, disruption, and desperation. The effects of these events were felt by large populations and entire regions, showing just how widespread they were.

As previously stated, famines were not rare occurrences and were, in fact, quite common. In Genesis 41, God revealed to Pharaoh through a series of dreams that a seven-year famine would follow seven years of prosperity. Joseph's interpretation of Pharaoh's dreams suggested that the years of famine would be so great that the people of Egypt would forget all the prosperity they had previously enjoyed. The famine would bring ruin to the land. It would be so severe that people would forget what it was like to have good years.

The question arises of what happens when the things you have relied on run out. What do you do when the tough seasons cause the good memories to fade away? When the good days no longer outweigh the bad, how do you survive?

Famines were frequently caused by droughts, among other natural causes and economic crises. Knowing this, it is intriguing that the famine Isaac faced, despite its severity, did not have any impact on the flow of water. Although Isaac and his servants had to endure a famine, they had no trouble finding water. But the water was discovered in particular locations, not just anywhere.

One of the places where Isaac and his servants found water was Gerar. Gerar is the place where Abraham dug wells during his lifetime. With famine comes suffering, and with suffering, opportunity. The opportunity to unearth what is already present. The opportunity to revisit an age-old provision and leverage what is left. The opportunity to grasp the generational provision ordained by God.

So, how do succeeding generations endure famine? By re-digging the wells.

> *"When Isaac planted his crops that year, he harvested a hundred times more grain than he planted, for the Lord blessed him. He became a very rich man, and his wealth continued to grow. He acquired so many flocks of sheep and goats, herds of cattle, and servants that the Philistines became jealous of him. So, the Philistines filled up all of Isaac's wells with dirt. These were the wells that had been dug by the servants of his father, Abraham. He reopened the wells his father had dug, which the Philistines had filled in after Abraham's death. Isaac also restored the names Abraham had given them."* - Genesis 26:12-15, 18

GOING FURTHER THAN YOUR FATHER

The foresight and hard work of Abraham in digging wells proved to be a significant factor in ensuring Isaac's survival during a period of famine. The wells symbolized generational provision, as God knew ahead of time that the famines would occur. However, while the wells gave him a starting point, they were not the end. He re-dug them, but his survival would necessitate more than what was handed down to him by his father. Isaac not only restored his father's wells but expanded his work by digging more wells on his journey. For him, this was more than just a physical journey—it was a symbolic representation of his spiritual path.

As with each preceding generation, Isaac went a step further than his father. Taking an extra step forward does not nullify the previous steps, rather it acknowledges that each generation's steps form part of a greater journey. Terah's footsteps served as a foundation for Abraham's, underscoring the significance of those who have come before us in shaping the course of our lives. Isaac followed the example of his father Abraham, who had gone a step further than his own father Terah, and took it even further. The God of Abraham, who was previously known as such, would thereafter be identified as the God of both Abraham *and* Isaac.

Generational provision is a fruit of generational faith. The fruit of being able to provide for future generations is rooted in the faith that is passed down through multiple generations. The reason Isaac had wells to re-dig was because Abraham had already dug them. The fact that Abraham had already dug the wells meant that Isaac did not have to start from scratch. The establishment of the covenant with Isaac was dependent on the obedience of Abraham. God even stated this in verse 5 of Genesis 26 when he said, "I will do this because Abraham listened to me and obeyed all my requirements, commands, decrees, and instructions." The obedience displayed by one generation had a lasting impact on the blessing that the next generation received.

Chapter 11 of Hebrews provides an in-depth review of how faith has been demonstrated by numerous individuals throughout history, starting with Abel and concluding with the martyrs of the New Testament. The acts of faith mentioned are not independent instances that impact just one person, but they are all interrelated and together form a cohesive fabric of faith. The chapter ends strongly with these words:

> "Not one of these people, even though their lives of faith were exemplary, got their hands on what was promised. God had a better plan for us: that their faith and our faith would come together to make one completed whole, their lives of faith not complete apart from ours." - Hebrews 11:39-40 (MSG)

The faith of your ancestors is an integral part of your own faith and without it, your faith is incomplete. The prayers of those who have gone before you are being fulfilled through your life, and the abundance you experience is a testament to generational faith. Just because it happens in your lifetime doesn't mean that it started or will end with you.

Every person's life is an integral piece of God's multi-generational plan. In Hebrews 12:2, Christ is identified as the author and finisher of our faith. He not only sets the perfect example of faith, but also represents the ultimate goal of faith.

It was through Christ's sacrifice and the fulfillment of the covenant that faith reached its culmination. However, we are experiencing an ongoing perfecting of faith in our lives presently. When we look at the bigger picture of Hebrews, we can understand that the faith authored by Christ is not only relevant to individuals but is also a faith that has a generational impact.

UP TO THE BRIM

The promise that God made to Isaac was fulfilled when he was blessed, and the enemy nations were powerless against it. The Philistines, motivated by envy over Isaac's prosperity, filled the wells that belonged to his father with dirt. This resulted in Isaac having to re-dig them. Although he re-dug his father's wells, it was not meant to be a tribute to his father. It was a stake of claim to the territory and a notice served to the Philistines that the wells and the land still belonged to his lineage.

Since the wells had reached a non-functional state with dirt up to the brim, Isaac could have opted not to re-dig them. Let's take a moment to think about how Isaac might have felt in this situation. Perhaps he felt frustrated as he thought about the amount of work that went into digging those wells, work that Abraham and his servants had tirelessly carried out. Perhaps he felt as though all the progress that had been made had been erased. He may have felt that he was now alone, with his father's footsteps faded and no clear direction to follow. Finally, he might have felt guilty or like he failed his father as the wells were now filled with dirt because of the Philistines' jealousy towards him.

Famines signify loss. With generational provision being a product of generational faith, Isaac may have felt a loss of purpose. This loss of purpose would not have been only of personal purpose but of the purpose of faith. Wells carried a meaning that went beyond economic provision. They were a direct reflection of the depth of faith that existed.

How do you deal with feeling like you're bearing the weight of your faith? When your beliefs are working against you, what do you do? What do you do when what worked for one generation does not work for you? How do you address the issue when the customs, traditions, or beliefs of one generation are no longer functional for the next generation? When the former provision that once helped your faith is obstructed, how do you maintain your faith?

Although the Philistines tried to frustrate him, Isaac knew that the wells were part of his inheritance and partial fulfillments to the covenant God had made.

The filling of the wells with dirt up to the brim was a symbolic act with several meanings attached to it. The unfolding of Genesis 26 reveals a pattern. Each well, except for one, came with opposition. Every time Isaac cleared a well, those who were residing on the land immediately asserted their ownership over it. The opposers aimed to distract Isaac by making him overly concerned with the wells, thus preventing him from noticing the bigger picture. It was a good thing that Isaac didn't restrict the blessing to only his father's wells. He kept digging.

· · • • • • • • · ·

Over the years, how have generations come to terms with this kind of loss? Where do those questions find *you*? Are the wells of your inner being filled with dirt up to the brim by the enemy?

Our lives can benefit greatly from the practice of examining our personal wells and assessing the areas that have been filled to the brim. You may have been given the responsibility of preserving your family's legacy, which can be a daunting task. Perhaps you were raised in a family where everyone pursued the same profession, and you feel pressure to continue the tradition.

Your confusion might deepen as you try to understand why your faith appears different now than it did in your childhood or from your parents' faith. When you encounter unfamiliarity on your faith journey, it can prompt you to question the validity of your faith. You may feel the urge to cling to outdated traditions and customs, fearing that seeking a personal connection with God is too risky.

The dirt that fills our wells up to the brim leaves us feeling purposeless, stagnant, and out of place. Doubts about our identity and worth can plague us, causing us to question our every move. If you're struggling to navigate this loss and the grief that accompanies, know that you are not alone. You may be wondering what to do when what is familiar is no longer functional. You have found yourself standing in front of wells that have been filled with dirt up to the brim, but all hope is not lost.

If you asked Isaac for a strategy, I believe he would say, "Keep digging". Esteem the previous wells and seize the opportunity of new wells in untouched ground. Understand that your provision and purpose extend beyond what has been inherited. You've been called to dig your own wells, too.

·····●·●····

Eventually, Isaac relocated to Beersheba and obtained rights to a new well. By continuing to dig, Isaac took ownership of his own life and journey. He faced opposition, but it was evident even to the enemy nation that God was on his side. In Genesis 26:28-29, they said:

> "'We can plainly see that the Lord is with you. So we want to enter into a sworn treaty with you. Let's make a covenant. Swear that you will not harm us, just as we have never troubled you. We have always treated you well, and we sent you away from us in peace. And now look how the Lord has blessed you!'"

Isaac's continued prosperity, despite being sent away by the Philistines, compelled their ruler to seek reconciliation and establish peace between them. God was blessing Isaac, just as He had promised.

The reason for God's blessing upon Isaac was not his infallible decision-making skills. Isaac's obedience to God, even in his weaknesses, led to him being blessed, and God remembered His covenant with him. As Solomon wrote in Proverbs 16:7, "When God approves of your life, even your enemies will end up shaking your hand" (MSG). God's favor towards Isaac had nothing to do with perfection and everything to do with covenant.

It is not a coincidence that Isaac moved to Beersheba. Beersheba is the very place where Abraham and Isaac journeyed to after being tested on Mount Moriah (Gen. 22:19). The location where Isaac was nearly sacrificed became a redemptive place for him as he encountered God, built an altar, and dug a well.

Isaac's seemingly scattered movements were, in reality, impeccably aligned with God's divine agenda. Some decisions made by older generations may not make sense to us today and may not have made sense to them either at that time. But in retrospect, God was guiding them according to a greater plan that they would only come to realize later on.

THE LOWEST PART

Ensuring that wells were functional involved a considerable amount of time, effort, and human resources. The people in the city used them daily, they were exposed to natural elements, and enemy nations could sabotage them. Whenever wells had to be re-dug, the lowest part of the structure was often the only part that remained intact, while the rest of the well was damaged by either human or natural factors.

As mentioned earlier in the book, wells carry a two-fold meaning: generational faith and inner life. The weight of sin and the harsh realities of life can erode our faith and inner lives. Daily, our faith is at risk of being shaken by things like injustices, divorce, terminal illnesses, losing a loved one, and economic crises.

As faith is passed from generation to generation, the foundation is there, but there is wear and tear affecting how each generation experiences God and navigates their faith journeys. Therefore, we should regularly examine the condition of our wells. It is our responsibility to ensure that the foundation of our inner lives, or the lowest part of our wells, remains intact.

I am reminded of Jesus' parable of the two builders in the Gospel of Matthew. The builder who is wise constructs a house on rock, while the foolish one constructs it on sand. In Luke's account, he makes a distinction between a house built on solid rock and one built on the ground without a foundation:

> "I will show you what it's like when someone comes to me, listens to my teaching, and then follows it. It is like a person building a house who **digs deep** and lays the foundation on solid rock. When the floodwaters rise and break against that house, it stands firm because it is well built. But anyone who hears and doesn't obey is like a person who builds a house right on the ground, without a foundation. When the floods sweep down against that house, it will collapse into a heap of ruins." - Luke 6:47-49

This parable implies that a builder must "dig deep" to ensure a solid foundation. The foundation's fortitude determines the severity of the storm's impact.

Shallow faith is a byproduct of impersonal faith. If your faith is disconnected, your foundation will be shallow. If your knowledge of God is purely theoretical and lacks experience, you haven't dug deep.

After hearing the Samaritan woman's testimony about her encounter with Jesus in John 4, many came to believe in Christ and His message. The people said to her, "We now believe not only because of your words; we have heard for ourselves, and we know that this man truly is the Savior of the world" (John 4:42).

A strong foundation demands an experiential faith. For a foundation to be stable, it must be grounded in personal experience. The faith of earlier generations may strengthen our belief in God, but there comes a time when we must encounter Him personally and form our own understanding of Him.

·········

A house on a rock is built on a firm foundation. If a well is dug deeply, the upper portions may be damaged, but the lowest part will remain unscathed. As Gordon MacDonald, author of *Ordering Your Private World*, described the inner life, the lowest part is "a quiet place where all is in order, a place from which comes the energy that overcomes turbulence and is not intimidated by it."[15]

Life can be tough, and it's easy for harsh realities to shake our faith. These realities are a humbling reminder that we are not as in control as we would like to believe we are. They remind us that even the best-laid plans can be disrupted, and we must learn to be flexible.

They also spoil our anticipation of what we're hoping for. We become apprehensive about looking forward to good things because we know that bad things are never too far away. When facing difficult circumstances, we tend to become self-absorbed and our interactions with others become less compassionate and empathetic. Rather than the sure evidence of what we are hoping for, faith becomes incriminating evidence of a God who is numb to our pain and whose palms are calloused from our neediness.

Life's tough realities can cause feelings of fear, bitterness, resentment, distrust, and shame. Our mindset can become trapped in poverty as these realities condition us to never expect more than what we have. Like the Israelites in the wilderness, we may be tempted to hoard leftovers of God's provision because maybe, just maybe, He won't provide tomorrow like He said.

One way we can renew our minds about our circumstances is by changing the way we see God. Builders who build their houses on rock and dig deep wells "will not be ashamed in the time of evil, and *in the days of famine they will have abundance*" (Ps. 37:19). They will be like trees who stand confidently when heat comes because their fruit remains (Jer. 17:7). They understand that fruit remains not because of their own sustaining abilities but God's.

So, how do we build houses on rocks? How do we dig wells that last? Instead of focusing on the external, our attention should be on the lower and more inner part. It is what MacDonald describes as "an inside-out matter, not an outside-in matter."[16] Building your life on the rock is an act of faith. Digging wells requires a deliberate approach and a defined purpose. In ancient times, the provision of wells was not solely based on the act of digging wells. The existence of a well would be pointless if it lacked functionality. To guarantee the functionality of your wells, you must restructure, reprioritize, and reorder your inner life. If you want to evaluate the functionality of your wells, you will have to go back to the foundation.

Famines have a way of forcing one to return to the basics. To this point, MacDonald writes:

> "When money is limited, one budgets. And when time is in limited supply, the same principle holds. The disorganized person must have a budgeting perspective. And that means determining the difference between the fixed—what one must do—and the discretionary—what one would like to do."[17]

Our inner wells suffer the consequences of spiritual famines, prompting us to differentiate between what is definite and what is open to change.

Scarcity breeds simplicity. In times of spiritual famines, the glitz and glam that typify worship experiences in a lot of our local churches cease to impress us anymore. When resources are scarce, the pursuit of worldly status and pleasures loses its appeal as it becomes clear that they are fleeting and short-lived. Scarcity puts things into perspective.

When famine strikes, we acknowledge that our plans and methods may not be enough, and we are open to new ideas. We evaluate our choices more critically, and our actions are more deliberate. We become selective about the relationships we invest in, choosing those that provide us with strength and nourishment. We no longer turn to God as our last resort in times of crisis. We shift our focus to the inner part. We begin again our Bible plans, seek counsel from spiritual leaders or mentors, value the wisdom of our elders, and make a conscious effort to set aside time for prayer and devotion in our busy week. However, our focus on the inner parts should not be limited to times of crisis but should be a constant priority.

·············

Throughout our life journey, we are given blessings and opportunities by God that we can use to make a difference in our lives and the lives of others. Despite our efforts to accumulate wealth, climb the corporate ladder, or make a difference in our communities here on earth, it's not for the purpose of having an impressive resume to present to God in heaven. Heaven won't be about us, and to be honest, neither is this life. This explains why it's so hard to find our life's purpose without God.

God has granted us the ability to work together with Him. He has partnered with us to carry out His divine purposes on earth. If we wish to see God's heavenly will come to fruition on earth, we must keep in mind that this life is fleeting, and we should live our lives as if we are not the focal point.

Before we can even think about building our houses on rocks and digging our wells deep, we need to lay a strong foundation of faith that will serve as the bedrock of our endeavors. If we want to establish a solid foundation for our beliefs, we need to look to God, and when examining our faith, we should turn it inside-out.

THE GOD OF ISAAC

When confronted with loss and forced to adapt to a simpler lifestyle due to scarcity, Isaac discovered the importance of digging deep wells. He dug wells, with both mundane and divine purposes, that would be inherited by his own sons.

Each generation has its own way of discovering and experiencing God. Over the course of his life, Isaac was able to cultivate important virtues like obedience, wisdom, and humility. While Isaac was first acquainted with the God of his father Abraham, it was through his own journey that he came to experience Him on a personal level.

On Mount Moriah, he had an opportunity to see how God provides for those who trust in Him. The demonstration of faith did not end there as he also saw the fruit of his father's confidence in God's ability to resurrect him if it became necessary to make a sacrifice (Heb. 11:19). It was there that he witnessed provision when logic dictated there should have been none.

He saw God's hand in his father's servant finding him a wife, just like how the servant prayed for. The God of Isaac revealed Himself as One who values our whole selves, not just our worship and service to Him. He is invested in every aspect of our lives, even down to the details of our relationships and the timing of them. Isaac saw God as a practical provider, wise counselor, and merciful rewarder of obedience.

As we will see in the next chapter, Gen Xers were introduced to and came to faith in the God of the Boomers. However, they discovered that the religious practices and beliefs that guided Boomer individuals in their faith were not entirely applicable to individuals in Gen X.

Gen X Christians had faith upbringings similar to their parents', but they were able to develop their own individual relationships with God. By reclaiming old wells and digging new ones, Isaac built upon Abraham's faith rather than duplicating it. As Isaac dug up his father's wells once more and took faith to the next level, Generation X also uncovered the inner wells inherited from the Boomers and acquired their own insight and acquaintance with God.

Chapter Four

GEN X

The forgotten middle child of generations.

Those born between 1965-1983 make up Generation X. This generation finds itself in the middle of two prominent generations, Boomers and Millennials. Similarly, Isaac is wedged between the father of many nations (Abraham) and the father whose sons became leaders of the twelve tribes of Israel (Jacob).

The story of Abraham's life is introduced in the closing of chapter 11 and then covered in detail from chapters 12 to 22. Jacob's life story is narrated from chapters 27 to 33. Genesis has many chapters, but only one of them, namely chapter 26, is entirely devoted to Isaac and his journey. This may cause one to overlook or underestimate the significance of his story. As demonstrated in the previous chapter, however, Isaac's role in fulfilling God's generational plan and promise was just as vital as Abraham's and Jacob's. The same thing can be said of Generation X.

Compared to earlier generations, Gen Xers were exposed to more divorce, single-parent households, and dual-income families. As latchkey kids, they had minimal adult supervision and were forced to prove their independence early on. This generation's worldview was largely shaped by events such as the Fall of the Berlin Wall, the Jonestown Massacre, 9/11, the Great Recession, the Watergate Scandal, the AIDS crisis, and the first Gulf War.

Gen Xers' mistrust of authority figures in political and spiritual domains is not surprising given the history of international crises, invasions, assassinations, and cults. Because of the injustices that their parents had to face and the time it took to see any real change, many individuals from Generation X grew up with a deep-seated skepticism towards the law. They grew up devoted to the faith but distrustful of authority.

When they became adults, they were tasked with the responsibility of providing for their children's financial needs and looking after their aging parents. Their reputation as self-reliant, critical thinkers with incredible resilience precedes them.

These traits have been key to their success, as they can navigate challenges and overcome obstacles with ease. Self-reliance is deeply ingrained in them, allowing them to be independent and capable individuals. Additionally, critical thinking is a skill they constantly rely on, enabling them to approach problems in a strategic and effective way. Lastly, their resilience has helped them push through difficult times and emerge stronger on the other side.

Boomers played by the rules. Gen X found some exceptions to the rules. Individuals belonging to this generation delayed marriage and childbearing to put their personal growth and development first. They were the first to recognize the importance of balancing work and personal life, perhaps because they witnessed the negative impact of their parents' workaholic tendencies on family life.

In response to the high demand for family-friendly schedules, the Federal Employees Part-time Career Employment Act of 1978 was signed into law to provide part-time hours and job sharing for employees. In 1994, President Clinton released a memorandum that directed institutions and organizations to establish flexible work arrangements.

Flexibility was important for Gen Xers, as it allowed them to not only spend more time with family but also pursue higher education. The emphasis placed by this generation on education is unmistakable, as they have surpassed all previous generations with the highest rate and level of education in the United States. They had a sense of pride in taking ownership of their lives and reclaiming control, which they believed their parents had deprived them of during their upbringing.

INNER WELLS

Writings of notable authors, including John Piper, C. S. Lewis, Charles Spurgeon, Rick Warren, Joyce Meyer, and Joel Osteen, are regarded as among the most influential for Generation X and captured the spirit of the time. The list of Christian authors born in Generation X includes Priscilla Shirer, Chrystal Evans Hurst, Tish Harrison Warren, Lysa TerKeurst, and Kate Bowler. The works of Gen X Christian authors have inspired readers through their emphasis on the importance of prayer, taking responsibility for one's life, maximizing one's potential, practicing spiritual authority, and exercising spiritual gifts.

The achievements of individuals in Generation X have been measured against the socioeconomic legacies of their Boomer parents. Keeping with the metaphor of wells, Gen Xers' success has been determined by the extent to which they have re-dug their parents' wells. Despite this, Gen Xers preferred to dig their own wells. It was paramount to them to build a legacy unique to them, not a duplicate of what they had received.

The exploration of faith in Generation X revealed two themes that played a significant role in shaping their spiritual, social, and economic outlooks. They pulled water from their inner wells using these themes as their buckets.

IDENTITY

First is identity. For individuals of the X generation, the process of discovering their identity and purpose involved the exploration of societal roles, careers, education, and spiritual gifts. While functionality was a key consideration, these matters were much more complex and multifaceted. They helped answer the question: What is my purpose in life?

As Gen Xers became adults and started their own families, their roles were directly tied to their faith and spiritual standing with God. Was it possible to be the best at everything all the time? The societal roles and expectations that were placed upon them were unrelenting, forcing Gen X individuals to run on the wheel of life without respite and with no chance of escape. Nonetheless, these roles were considered by them as an essential element of intentional living, and it provided them with ways to identify themselves apart from their parents.

In their quest for autonomy, they looked for opportunities to approach relationships, marriage, parenthood, and faith differently. They yearned for independence and self-direction in their homes, spirituality, political opinions, and workplaces. The movements that transpired during this generation's upbringing are a testament to this.

Spiritual gifts were also a way in which Gen X Christians learned to identify themselves. Don and Katie Fortune's *Discover Your God-Given Gifts* was published in 1987 and became a primary resource in many Christian homes and congregations. Gen Xers went a step further in their exploration and encouragement of spiritual gifts. To them, spiritual gifts were not only reserved for spiritual leaders and authority figures. They were available to everyone. In accordance with Martin Luther's teachings on the priesthood of all believers, God has given everyone spiritual gifts, and we can use these gifts within and beyond the church. Identifying their unique spiritual gifts was one step on Gen X individuals' journey towards living autonomously.

Gen Xers wanted their faith to stand on its own, separate from their parents'. Bored with being looked over, they were willing to go to any extent to assert their individuality and take back control of their lives. The weight of hardship had taken its toll on them, and they were ready for a change. They envisioned a better future for themselves and their communities and were determined to make it a reality. In efforts to meet practical needs of congregants and community members, they employed their spiritual gifts and served in para-church organizations, recognizing a need for action where their parents' generation had fallen short.

ESCAPE

"I did discover that the prosperity gospel encourages people (especially its leaders) to buy private jets and multimillion-dollar homes as evidence of God's love. But I also saw the desire for escape. Believers wanted an escape from poverty, failing health, and the feeling that their lives were leaky buckets. Some people wanted Bentleys but more wanted relief from the wounds of their past and the pain of their present. People wanted salvation from bleak medical diagnoses; they wanted to see God rescue their broken teenagers or their misfiring marriages."[18] - Kate Bowler

The second is escape—the way Gen Xers maneuvered through life's disruptions. Televangelists in the 1980s helped to spread the influence of the prosperity gospel. This "gospel" proposes that faith and prosperity are intertwined in a transactional manner. If you do x, God will do y. If you do not do x, God will not do y. Thus, suffering is avoidable and completely consequential. The disciples in John 9 were motivated by this same belief system when they asked if a man's blindness was due to his sin or his parents' sins. There's no room for blanks in the prosperity gospel. Every problem has a solution and every question has an answer. If it's not good, it's not God. God wants nothing more than for His people to have wealth, happiness, and victory. Suffering is only a detour on the journey to a life of abundance.

The prosperity gospel itself, as Bowler points out, isn't infatuating. What's appealing is the idea of getting away, or escaping. When you have experienced suffering firsthand and have inherited the consequences of decisions made by previous generations, the idea of prosperity doesn't seem all that bad. In its purest form, it is our heart's plea like Moses' in Psalm 90:15 when he said: "Make us glad for as many days as you have afflicted us, for as many years as we have seen trouble" (NIV). It feels as though we are entitled to prosperity when we contemplate the weighty cross that we have been assigned to bear.

It is reassuring to know that we do not need to rely on a prosperity gospel when we have a loving God who wishes to give us good things. A gospel of prosperity is pointless, as prosperity is only meaningful if provided by God. It is the pre-existing goodness of the God who grants them that makes the things we strive for good. The goodness that we encounter in life is not simply a result of the material things we acquire, but it is rather a manifestation of God's kindness, and His unyielding commitment to grant us His blessings. So then, the problem is not with the desire for good, but with the desire for good that excludes God.

One problem with the prosperity gospel is that it encourages a sense of entitlement in those who follow it. When we experience good things, we often begin to believe that we deserve them and that they should be a constant in our lives. This can become a condition that we use to determine whether we will continue to serve God. We make our loyalty to God contingent on whether He provides us with what we desire.

As much as we want perfect lives that only attract good things, look at the news and you'll see that it is practically impossible. The fact that we, as humans, have co-agency, free will, and a natural tendency to sin, means that we must be ready to take ownership and accept responsibility for the part we have played in the state of the world. God has made it clear that His plans for us involve prosperity, not harm. However, this prosperity is on His terms, at the time of His choosing, and based on how we steward the free will we've been granted.

CONTEMPORIZING CHRISTIANITY

Despite the introduction of alternative spiritual options during the New Age Movement, some Gen X individuals still found themselves unsatisfied. While they were open to exploring alternative religions, they ultimately did not find the answers they were seeking.

They made their way back to Jesus, but with a different approach. As mentioned earlier, famines tend to strip away the unnecessary and bring us back to the basics. They hoped to eliminate suffering and legalism by placing Jesus Christ and the gospel message at the center.

Started by youth on the West Coast, the Jesus Movement rapidly spread throughout the nation, inspiring many. The movement had followers from late Boomers to young adults in Generation X between the late 1960s and late 1980s. The primary objectives of this movement were to understand Jesus from the angles of peace, love, and inclusivity. These young people sought alternative ways of life that were countercultural to their upbringing and their parents' traditional ways. They were ready to challenge the status quo.

The Seeker-Sensitive Movement, the Emergent Church Movement, New Calvinism, and the Christian Rock and Contemporary Christian music genres all trace back to the Jesus Movement. The Seeker-Sensitive Movement involved an evangelistic technique that centered on creating an attractive gospel and Christian lifestyle that would appeal to church attendees. Its primary goal was to lure people with songs, language, and messages that were precisely what they wanted to hear. These songs and messages failed to capture the weight of religious commitment and the sacrifice it entails.

Seeker churches made a distinction between ministry to the saved and ministry to the unsaved. Small groups were reserved for church members. Sunday services were designed to cater to those who were not regular churchgoers, hoping to attract them with an easy-going environment. They limited sharing the truth about Christian life and accountability to small groups only. It was considered inappropriate to expose the unsaved to songs and sermons about suffering and sin. The gospel needed to be presented in a fairytale manner to bring in the unsaved. Only after committing their lives to Christ would individuals learn the truth about the Gospel and Christian living.

The Emergent Church Movement prioritized subjectivity instead of facts, endorsed relative truth, and advocated for the church to evolve as culture changed. Above all else, the church was expected to resemble the culture.

New Calvinism was unique in its ability to unite people from diverse denominations and ethnic backgrounds around a shared mission. Its goal was to bring Old Calvinistic teachings and ideologies up to date with modern times. All these movements have transformed the American church, Christian music, and para-church organizations in ways that are still visible today.

Among the findings of the religious study conducted by the Pew Research Center in 2014, there was one that was particularly noteworthy. Although individuals belonging to Generation X placed a high value on prayer and engaged in it daily, they were not habitual attendees of corporate prayer meetings.[19] The study's results suggest that Generation X individuals followed in the footsteps of their parents' generation by re-digging wells that included spiritual disciplines, attending church, and seeking to know God in a more experiential way.

But they also attempted to develop a personalized faith by digging their own wells. Once they became adults, many Gen Xers shied away from corporate gatherings and expressions of worship, even though they were forced to attend while growing up. Their obligations to the church during their formative years did not match their desired approach to raising their own children. Although they recognized the advantages of faith and acknowledged that involvement in the local church is beneficial, their experiences with church as children left many of them burned out and so they made a conscious decision to approach things differently as adults.

THE GOD OF GENERATION X

Generation X individuals understood that to move a step further than their parents' generation, they would have to be willing to do things differently. Not everyone stayed true to their faith, but those who did passed on wells to the next generation.

The faith of Generation X echoes our desire for a relatable Savior and a faith that can be practically applied to our multifaceted lives. It underscores the importance of letting God's voice have more weight in shaping our identity than the culture's. Our true identity and purpose can only be known in relation to God, and as we seek to do things differently, we must be cautious not to deviate too far from the principles we have been taught.

Jacob and the Millennials will be the focus of our exploration in Part III. We will explore their assignment to move beyond the wells while honoring the wells that were passed down to them. The upcoming chapter will closely examine Jacob's journey and the spiritual ramifications of the events that transpired throughout his life.

Part III. Moving Beyond the Wells

Chapter Five

JACOB

J acob was the twin of Esau, the son of Isaac and Rebekah, and the grandson of Abraham and Sarah.

His name means "one who follows on another's heel" because he was born holding on to the heel of his brother. It also means "supplanter", one who supersedes or takes the place of, often through coercion or trickery. This label associated with his name remained present throughout his life. We find the genesis of his story in Genesis 27.

It has been taught that Jacob's behavior towards his brother Esau, father Abraham, and uncle Laban was consistent with the implications of his name. However, with careful observation, it becomes apparent that Jacob was never the initiator of the deception.

According to Genesis 25, Jacob did not use trickery to obtain Esau's birthright. At the time, Esau thought it had no value, so he willingly gave it over. There was no ulterior motive, only a decision that Esau would eventually regret and hold resentment toward Jacob for.

Regarding the blessing of the firstborn in Genesis 27, deceiving his father was never Jacob's intention. Discussion of the birthright occurred when he was not even present in the room. His mother, Rebekah, shared a plan with him after eavesdropping on Isaac's talk with Esau. Due to her preference for Jacob over Esau, she devised a plan and took responsibility for any aftermath that would result.

It is rarely mentioned, but Jacob made efforts to persuade his mother that her plan would be unsuccessful and that his father would end up cursing him instead of blessing him. Despite his reluctance, Rebekah insisted that he carry out the task and assured him that she would take the curse upon herself if need be.

· · · ● · ● ● · · ·

It's possible that Rebekah's insistence on Jacob receiving Abraham's blessing was connected to a prophecy she received while pregnant with the twins. Genesis 25 reveals that Jacob and Esau were hostile towards each other in the womb, and Rebekah prayed to God for insight. The Lord revealed to her that her younger son would have power over the older one, and their nations would be adversaries from the beginning.

Rebekah's plan was clearly manipulative, but it also seemed to be driven by her desire to find her place in the prophecy's fulfillment. Supposing the Lord's words were truthful, and the heritage of Abraham and Isaac was to be given to the succeeding generation, Jacob *had* to receive the blessing.

Rebekah might have believed that by taking action, she was helping God out. But even if she hadn't been granted foreknowledge, the blessing of Jacob was already in God's plan before his birth, and it was bound to happen.

To us, Rebekah's act was manipulative, but in reality, it is a perfect illustration of the complexity of intergenerational faith and blessings. Throughout history, humans have endeavored to assist God in implementing His intergenerational plan.

There are pressures within families for everyone to pursue the same career path, attend the same school, have the same number of children, or marry the same type of people. But the blessing is not linked to any of our efforts. Before we decide to participate, it has already been set in motion.

A word of counsel to younger generations: older generations are not always seeking to control our lives more than they are attempting to find their place in the fulfillment of God's plan for us. To ensure prophecies about their children come to pass, many individuals feel they must take an active role in bringing them to fruition.

They take it upon themselves to ensure that your life unfolds according to their expectations, and they hold you accountable for how you steward it. Although their intentions may be good, those responsibilities are not theirs to take on.

Our lives are our own responsibility, and older generations must have faith that God is guiding us every step of the way, just as He has done with them. They must also accept that not every promise is intended for them to witness firsthand.

Jacob had a chance to make his own decision but succumbed to the pressure to act on Rebekah's anxiety. Who or what have you allowed to influence *your* decisions?

·· • • •• • • •· ·

By following through with the plan, Jacob secured the blessing that was originally intended for the firstborn. Rebekah, concerned for Jacob's safety, advised him to leave home after his brother threatened to kill him. Before his departure, Jacob received another blessing from his father. Afterwards, Abraham instructed Jacob to stay with his uncle Laban and to marry one of Laban's daughters.

A well is introduced in Jacob's story as the place where he met his wife, Rachel. His love for her was so fervent that he agreed to work for seven years to receive her hand in marriage, and to him, the years felt like a handful of days.

After seven years, he approached Laban with excitement, ready to take Rachel as his bride. Laban agreed, but when night came, he tricked Jacob by sending Leah instead of Rachel. Jacob woke up the next morning shocked to discover that he had married the wrong sister. When he approached Laban about it, he was told that it was against their tradition to give the youngest daughter in marriage before the older one. Laban could have shared this with Jacob before the seven years of labor, but he opted to deceive him instead.

Making matters more complicated, Laban told Jacob that if he still wished to marry Rachel, he would have to work another seven years. Jacob worked for seven additional years, took Rachel as his second bride, and both wives bore children who ultimately became the leaders of the twelve tribes of Israel. His unwavering dedication to Rachel is commendable, but I can't help but wonder if there were moments of disappointment and bitterness, even though he loved her.

We have labeled Jacob as the deceitful trickster, but who could *Jacob* trust? His parents' unfair favoritism between him and his brother caused a significant divide in their family. His mother was willing to go to extreme lengths, risking his life and family ties, to achieve her goals. Then, he complied with his father's orders to marry one of his uncle's daughters, but was tricked into marrying the wrong one and cheated out of twenty years' worth of wages. Sure, Jacob had a predisposition for deception, but we cannot ignore the fact that he was also wronged.

· · · ● · ● · ● · · ·

Jacob's reputation for trickery extends beyond his immediate family. This is evidenced by the account in Genesis 30 where he allegedly deceived his uncle Laban and took possession of his finest cattle. Although Jacob had been working diligently for Laban, he wasn't receiving fair wages in return. However, Laban was experiencing an abundance of blessings because of Jacob's hard work and dedication.

Jacob had reached a point where he wanted to support his own family and earn his own income. So, Laban inquired about what he wanted as payment. Jacob made a deal with him to claim ownership of all the black, speckled, and spotted sheep and goats.

He said to his uncle, "In the future, when you check on the animals you have given me as my wages, you'll see that I have been honest. If you find in my flock any goats without speckles or spots, or any sheep that are not black, you will know that I have stolen them from you" (Gen. 30:33). To me, this action aligns more with accountability and integrity rather than the mischievous nature of a natural-born trickster.

Laban agreed to Jacob's request, but he went out that same day and removed all the goats and sheep that now belonged to Jacob and gave them to his sons (vv. 35-36). Not only was Jacob's flock now in Laban's sons' possession, but if he wanted to reclaim his flock, he would have to travel three days to retrieve them.

Once again, the role of the trickster did not fall on Jacob. It was Laban. And as a result of his uncle's trick, Jacob was left with no other choice but to come up with a creative solution. To avoid being accused of stealing by his uncle, he needed to come up with a plan to get the flock he had agreed to provide for his family. Rather than mixing his flock with Laban's as he usually did, he bred his own speckled and spotted flock. Laban's deception forced Jacob to think creatively about how to support his family.

As alluded to by Jacob in Genesis 31, this creative strategy was divine provision. He told his wives about a dream in which an angel of God spoke to him. The angel informed him that the successful breeding of the flock was a result of divine intervention, as the same God who had revealed Himself to Jacob at Bethel was aware and took account of Laban's mistreatment towards him over the years. Jacob had left his homeland alone, but he had divine company.

In the same chapter, Laban's sons started complaining about Jacob's wealth, which led to a sudden change in Laban's attitude towards him. But the Lord said to Jacob, "I will be with you", and He instructed him to return to the land of his forefathers to live there.

When Laban realized that Jacob had left without informing him, Laban set out in hot pursuit to catch up with him. He had every intention of harming Jacob, but God intervened and commanded him not to lay a finger on him. When Laban arrived at Jacob's campsite, they aired their grievances and made a pact.

THE WRESTLING

God had a strategic reason for sending Jacob back to his homeland. He knew that Jacob would have to pass through Edom, the territory which belonged to his brother, Esau. Genesis 32 describes how Jacob prepared for this encounter. He sent messengers ahead of him only to find out that Esau was already on his way... with an army of 400 men. Jacob was afraid for his life and did all he could to appease Esau.

Later, with the night at its peak, we discover him wide awake and restless. Without revealing the reason, he left his family and belongings, crossing the river to the other side.

Jacob found himself alone on one side of the river with his family and possessions on the other.

The man Jacob stumbled upon next was none other than God Himself. Despite differing opinions on whether it was an angel or a human figure, it was a manifestation of God. The timing of this encounter is noteworthy, as it was when Jacob was alone and had exhausted all efforts to ensure his safety. God orchestrated the encounter to happen when Jacob was at his most vulnerable. Jacob was standing at a crossroads between his past struggle with Laban and an impending battle with Esau. However, God wanted Jacob to realize that the actual struggle was within himself.

As with Jacob, God often appears to us when we have no other sources of comfort. When was the last time God got *you* alone? Slowed you down long enough to catch His words? Stripped away everything you've attached to your identity, forcing you to confront *you*?

If we do not deliberately decelerate, life will do it for us. Maybe with a phone call in the middle of the night. A visit to the emergency room. A family crisis. A financial setback. A serious illness or an unfavorable doctor's report. Anything that breaks into our routine and forces us to stop and pay attention. Like Jacob did, we often encounter God in places we never thought to look. He is where we did not expect Him to be. We find Him in places where we wouldn't normally seek Him out.

· • · • •·•·• • ··

In this unexpected meeting with God, Jacob wrestled with Him all night long, refusing to let go until He blessed him. Finally, with a simple touch, the man dislocated Jacob's thigh. Physiologists propose that the rectus femoris, or thigh, is one of the most powerful muscles in the human body, depending on the strength measure. *Shoq*, the Hebrew word for thigh, is a metaphor for a runner's muscular strength and self-assurance. By touching Jacob's thigh, the man was crippling Jacob at the point of his greatest strength.

What is the area where you find it hardest to put your trust in God? Where do you feel you lack faith? Which aspect of your life do you feel the most in control of? Can you identify an area of your life where you've become too self-sufficient? What about self-reliant? Our faith is often shaken when we feel like we've lost control, and God meets us right there.

In biblical times, people granted blessings to one another. Being blessed was not a feeling, sensation, or assumption. Instead, there was always concrete indication, or a material transaction made to represent one's favor.

Jacob was a wealthy man whom God had blessed during his lifetime. However, he was estranged from his family of origin, had made some choices he regretted, and his relationship with his extended family was not ideal. The assumption may have been that if he had enemies, then God must have been dissatisfied with him as well. It was challenging for Jacob, as well as for other individuals throughout Scripture, to dissociate enmity with people from enmity with God. So, he clung tightly to God, just as he had clung to his brother's heel, unwilling to release until he received a blessing.

Jacob said, "I won't let go until you bless me." I find this interesting, considering that the Lord had already blessed him—in the traditional way, at least. He had made Jacob and all those around him wealthy. But remember, Jacob left his family and livestock on the other side of the river. I think that action symbolized that there must be more to blessing than wealth and accumulation. There must be more to our identities than what we do and what we possess. Thus, it is possible that Jacob's words were not an insistence on acquiring more material things, but a plea for a spiritual blessing. Jacob had received blessings inherited from and bestowed by his father, but now he was seeking a blessing from God directly—a blessing that would run deep.

The blessing Jacob prevailed for did not come in the form he expected. Scripture is vague about what it entailed. All we know is that it was a physically altering, name changing blessing.

It's easy to overlook the true meaning of generational blessing for utility, limiting it to what we have to show for rather than who we are. What Jacob realized was that the blessing of most importance wasn't the natural one spoken by his father, Isaac, for the firstborn. The birthright and material possessions didn't contain it. It was contained within the spiritual inheritance and impartation he received while wrestling. The true blessing extended beyond the wells. It was not the tangible wealth given by humans, but the intangible inheritance bestowed by God.

DISPLACED IDENTITY

An overarching motif in Jacob's life was the displacement of his identity. From birth, his name was determined by his actions, and his actions were a reflection of his identity. He *was* his behavior. As mentioned in their respective chapters, both Abraham and Isaac tricked the Egyptians by presenting their wives as their sisters. Were Jacob a trickster, it would have been consistent with the family pattern. But while trickery was a family trait, Jacob was the one who was labeled for it. For Abraham and Isaac, trickery was an action, a tool even, but for Jacob, it was his identity.

I waited until now to bring up the fact that God established His covenant with Jacob in Genesis 28. I did this because the typical narrative of Jacob's story might lead one to assume that God established His covenant with Jacob *after* his name change. However, the covenant was not displaced; Jacob's identity was. And his displacement began the moment he was labeled.

The lesson that Jacob's experience teaches us is that there is a contrast between identity displacement and being out of covenant. Jacob was in covenant before he was renamed Israel, and before he reconciled with Esau. In the wrestling, Jacob was still in covenant, and the covenant was unaffected by whether he prevailed. This highlights the generational continuity of faith and the plan of God. The covenant did not start with Jacob, and it did not start with you.

JACOB'S WELL

Scholars believe that Jacob's Well was most likely dug following Jacob's reconciliation with Esau. It was located on a plot of land that Jacob had purchased near Shechem and Sychar. As narrated in John 4, this is the well where Jesus sat and talked with the Samaritan woman. We will discuss the significance of this in chapter 7.

THE GOD OF JACOB

Jacob's journey with God was filled with strategic encounters. We see God instructing him throughout his life and giving him innovative strategies to move the intergenerational plan forward. These strategies had a dual benefit of fulfilling God's plan and providing Jacob with the resources to support his family. As Jacob's relationship with God deepened, he learned that He is the One who can answer prayers, perform miracles such as opening barren wombs, and offer protection against the enemy.

God revealed Himself to Jacob as One who sees and acts in in the face of injustice. Being aware of Laban's unfair treatment towards Jacob, He made sure that the flock was successfully bred, which led to Jacob's prosperity. This is an encouraging reminder to us that God has not turned a blind eye or deaf ear to the chaos created by humans in our nation and in the world.

Millennials are the last generation we will discuss in this book. The stories of their lives are still being written, history is still unfolding, and their faith is still taking shape. Known for their non-traditional approach and embrace of societal labels, Millennials have placed God in a box with everything else. Perhaps He is just as unreliable as people are. Perhaps faith is nothing more than wishful thinking. Perhaps there is a better, less expensive alternative to Christian living. Many Millennials are in search of an effortless Christianity like their parents experienced during the Jesus Movement. Some feel that the Jesus their parents and grandparents followed is outdated, and that Christian living is no longer relevant.

Despite having more luxuries and freedom than previous generations, they are more discontented, depressed, and discouraged than their parents and grandparents were at their age. Like Jacob, Millennials are dealing with identity displacement and wrestling in their faith. Bringing attention to these struggles is critical, as the faith of future generations, including Generation Z, will be shaped by how Millennials handle their inherited faith.

Chapter Six

MILLENNIALS

T *he rebellious generation.*

Those born between 1984 and 2000 are identified as Millennials. This generation is also known as Gen Me, Gen Y, and Echo Boomers. The childhood and adulthood of this generation have seen significant events such as 9/11, the Iraq/Afghanistan War, the Great Recession, the election of the first African American president, and the Sandy Hook Massacre. While history continues to unfold for this generation and those to follow, the events that have already occurred have left a lasting impression on their perspective on life and society.

This is the generation I belong to. According to Psychology Today, success is an immense pressure for Millennials. This pressure is the driving force behind our courage, innovation, creativity, and entitlement. We are striving to do our best given the circumstances of the times in which we find ourselves, much like every other generation before us.

Due to the fluctuations in the economy and the rise of inflation, the process of securing wealth through traditional means such as home ownership and established careers has become less streamlined than it was in the past. As we push the limits, we face economic challenges that previous generations did not have to. The conventional milestones of success are nearly unattainable for the younger generations.

It seems like every day the cost of living goes up a little more. This reality holds true not only financially but also mentally and emotionally. Millennials are struggling with higher rates of depression and anxiety compared to our parents and grandparents at our age.

Despite our privilege, Millennials feel unsupported. We're prioritizing our mental health by seeking therapy, but in doing so, we are breaking away from the values we grew up with—where everything was either taken to God or kept within the family. We are prioritizing our physical health, building reliance on medical professionals, scheduling our physical evaluations, and trusting medicine to perform its intended job. However, our attempts at taking care of our bodies are often met with ridicule, as if we don't have faith in God's ability to keep us healthy.

These days, things are moving faster than ever, and it's becoming increasingly difficult to navigate. We want to do life with others while still being true to ourselves. But our reliance on others to define our identity and purpose in life has left us with little confidence in our own intuition and decision-making abilities. The hope we were raised to believe in is slipping away, and with it, the faith of many Millennial individuals is dwindling.

The current state of our local churches is a cause for concern. Among Millennials, the sacredness of church leadership and sanctity of ministry are seldom upheld. The Levitical law of the Bible days was more than a set of rules. It served as a reminder of God's holiness, righteousness, and the high standards He expects from His people. To be in the vicinity of God and to engage in His ministry was a weighty responsibility.

Nowadays, local churches and their leaders are receiving more coverage in pop culture than ever before. Our pulpits are being filled with more talented, entrepreneurial enthusiasts than shepherds. Discipleship takes a back seat as church leaders aim to scale the church like a business. As a result, we are becoming increasingly disenchanted with the local church and ministry.

INNER WELLS

Regarding inner wells, a number of us have re-dug the wells of our parents and grandparents. Like the Boomers, we seek to know God through personal experience. What we're interested in is a God who practically affects our lives and the world around us, not just a theoretical one. Believing without any proof of our faith's impact is not enough for us.

Like Generation X, we are in search of our identity and striving for fulfillment in life. The pursuit of identity and fulfillment provides an avenue to escape the harsh societal conditions and resolve any internal dissonance we may be experiencing.

Our faith is a progression of the faith we were handed down. However, there are differences as the faith of Christians in our generation unfolds.

The Baby Boomers played by the rules. Generation X found some exceptions to the rules. Millennials disregard the rules entirely. Unlike our grandparents' generation, we are more creative than we are disciplined. Unlike our parents' generation, we are unwilling to sacrifice our individual values for conformity.

Since spirituality encompasses our whole lives, any spiritual discontentment we feel affects all other areas of our lives. Our pursuit of fulfillment is unwavering, and we refuse to stay in any churches, jobs, or relationships that fail to meet our expectations.

Our strengths include our courage to ask questions, stand up for injustices, and confront what we believe is wrong. While we should be proud of our drive, ambition, accountability, and self-advocacy, it's important to recognize our blind spots. The obstacle that poses the greatest threat is that we are a generation of great courage and little conviction. When our needs go unfulfilled, we seek to modify the Christian faith and local church to suit our preferences. We are quick to abandon our faith for broken wells.

LABELS

The extent of identity displacement experienced by Millennials has led researchers to question if we are the new Lost Generation. Similar to Jacob, we have been given labels, and those labels define our identities.

The local church played a vital role in shaping the identity and worldview of Christians in previous generations, providing them with a framework for understanding the world. They carried the insights they gained about themselves in the church with them as they engaged in society. On the other hand, the labels that Millennials use to identify themselves are a product of societal influence, and these labels are brought into the church.

········

Trickery was Abraham's and Isaac's mistake, but for Jacob, it was his identity. We, as Millennials, have been the target of judgment for matters that our parents and grandparents also had trouble with, but they did not voice them as frequently as we do. Our language has evolved, but our experiences are not entirely unique to our generation. As the writer of Ecclesiastes said, "History merely repeats itself. It has all been done before. Nothing under the sun is truly new. Sometimes people say, 'Here is something new!' But actually, it is old; nothing is ever truly new" (Ecc. 1:9-10).

Among all the generations, Millennials are feeling the most pressure to break the cycle of generational curses, as we have recognized the patterns and struggles for what they truly are. The issues of race, gender, sexuality, abuse, infidelity, injustice, and faith tradition are not new and have been present long before Millennials started emphasizing them. Throughout history, these undercurrents have always been present. The younger generations are just vocalizing it in a different way.

Labels have taken over our generation, but we are not the first to experience them. The 1900s marked the start of giving generations distinctive names, beginning with the Lost Generation. While previous generations have shunned labels, this generation seems to find comfort in them. We have allowed society to label us, but we have also internalized those labels and made them part of our identity and purpose. Society's labels have driven our generation to seek refuge in job titles, relationship statuses, and even ministry titles.

· · • • • • • · ·

Imagine I asked you to give me a brief introduction of yourself. What would you say? Societal conditioning would probably influence your response, leading you to mention your job title, years of experience, education, or professional background. You might even note any weekend volunteer work or participation in church-related activities as a bonus. But do people know you for who you are, or just for what you do?

How many people are privy to your purpose, your dreams and aspirations, your deepest fears, your greatest convictions, your desired legacy, or the questions that keep you awake at night? We may be skilled networkers, and our names may carry weight with a wide range of people. But do others *really* know us?

There is an unmistakable dissonance here, as being recognized by a multitude of people does not prevent us from having the highest rates of loneliness among all generations. The underlying issue lies in the reality that we are proximal but not relational. Being near each other is not the problem, our lack of a connection is. We would like to say that we are proximal, yet we have few genuine relationships to show for it.

Who can blame us, though? Social media has created a culture that values curated personas over authenticity, leading to a constant need to change to stay relevant. The rise of social media means that our online presence is often more important than our physical presence, and many people have more social connections online than in person. It has become increasingly effortless for individuals to isolate themselves from others and hide their true selves.

From fashion trends to technological advancements, every generation leaves its mark on society through the identity markers and status symbols they establish. For Boomers, it was work. For Gen X, it was education. For our generation, it is our reputation.

Some people view the use of labels as nothing more than a way to categorize and classify things into distinct groups. Others use these self-assigned titles to rebuild or establish their sense of self-worth. The use of labels and titles in society can perpetuate a sense of exclusivity and create barriers between individuals or groups who may not hold the same status or title. Understanding this, we can make sense of why certain cliques exist in some of our local communities and church congregations.

Identity crisis, which is a common phenomenon among Millennials, is having a profound impact on our ability to connect with God and establish a spiritual relationship. Some of us are searching for our identities and purposes in all the wrong places, and our understanding of God is as sure as our understanding of ourselves.

IDOLATRY

Christianity is losing its grip on the Millennial generation. The functions of the local church have changed from what they once were, and certain spiritual practices are no longer seen as necessary. This generation may believe in God, but they would much rather rely on themselves. The majority do not regularly attend church unless they benefitted from it in their upbringing, and they prefer not to be controlled by any authority figure, regardless of the setting.

Within our local churches, we have a lower view of authority than previous generations. For many Millennial Christian individuals, having a high regard for authority has been replaced with idolatry of either church leaders or of self. For some, pastors and spiritual leaders are no more messengers of God than they are celebrities. By the time congregants finish rolling out the red carpets for their leaders, there is little praise left for Christ.

To appear more approachable and relatable, church leaders have opted for a more casual worship experience. The outcome of this is that there is a lot of activity happening with little transformation taking place. In the absence of transformation, lingering uncertainties, doubts, and unresolved sin resurface after the service concludes.

Due to incidents of spiritual abuse, false teachings, and religious scandals, pastors and spiritual leaders have lost the respect of certain individuals. The Church's lack of transparency and accountability has led Millennials to conclude that it cannot be trusted. Millennial individuals who have witnessed the Church's scandals firsthand have lost faith in its credibility. For them, it is not mandatory to have a church or spiritual leaders because everyone has their own unique connection with God.

In their self-reliance, some Millennial individuals have become their *own* idols. Their ability to manifest their desires is the reason things happen for them. According to their belief, there is a power deep within us that holds the key to unlocking the secret of life. They are advocates for the regaining of control over one's own destiny and safeguarding one's energy from those who seek to sidetrack them. As far as they are concerned, a well is only worth drawing from if it serves their own interests. This may give a sense of self-empowerment and self-affirmation, but the fulfillment it provides is only temporary and short-lived. If we control our hearts, minds, and bodies, where does Christ make His home?

Both our reliance on labels and inclination to idolize stem from pride. This is to be expected since our generation is often referred to as entitled and self-absorbed. However, there is nothing new under the sun, including pride. Pride has been a thorn in humanity's side since the Garden of Eden. Jacob, who we identify with in our time, experienced many of the same difficulties we are encountering. He struggled with finding his place in his family, work, relationships, and living arrangements. He traveled far and wide, accumulated great wealth, and had a big family, yet he still could not shake the feeling of being unfulfilled.

THE WRESTLING

Jacob's restlessness and displacement reached their peak in a wrestling match that theologians have been pondering for centuries. As previously narrated, Jacob wrestled with God until the break of dawn. His wrestling was a physical battle, but for Millennials, it is a spiritual one. Though it may manifest physically at times, the heart of our wrestling is spiritual.

As a generation, we are wrestling in our faith. We struggle to find closure because we're unsure of how to come to terms with unanswered questions and, if we're brave enough to acknowledge it, unanswered prayers. While growing up, we had questions we were too afraid to ask our pastors or family members. Questions like: What happens when the outcome you prayed for doesn't come to pass? Does He not have the power and desire to heal us? Is He indifferent to the value of life? Does he punish innocent people with illness and suffering?

If you've ever held the hand of a loved one suffering from an illness, praying for their recovery, only to say goodbye to them forever, you understand the pain. The aftermath of losing a friend to suicide or senseless gun violence can leave you grappling with a range of emotions and thoughts. A financial crisis can leave you questioning everything, even if you thought you had your career and life in order. There are times in all our lives where we question whether it's better to lose faith than to keep facing disappointment.

As a generation, we are struggling to reconcile our beliefs with our experiences. For some, church is a place for wishful thinking, brimming with well-intentioned sayings that may aid us in confronting the world, but do not fully alleviate our distress. Death is a prime example. We are not interested in hearing that God needed our deceased loved ones more than we did or that He needed another flower in His garden. While it's comforting to believe that everything happens for a reason, we would have much rather they were healed on earth.

I am not ashamed to say that there have been many occasions on which I mourned as those who have no hope. Even though I wanted to hold on to hope, I couldn't find it... at least not in God. My hope was anchored in answers, healing, and rescuing. Not in God. During those times, I placed my hope in His performance rather than His character. I fixated my hope on His behavior rather than His essence. Influenced by the stories and experiences of my parents, grandparents, and other seasoned saints, I trusted Him to the extent to which He lived up to *their* testimonies of Him.

So, when I found myself in the midst of grief, I pointed fingers at Him. Every day, I was reminded of the darkness in the world as news of death, crime, and senseless violence dominated the media, and I questioned why He allowed it to happen. I couldn't help but feel betrayed by Him. As time went by, and as the disappointments piled up, my response to "God is good" grew fainter. Is He really good *all* the time?

The way we react to disappointment in our relationship with God is often a reflection of how we handle disappointment in our earthly relationships. It's common to attribute feelings of betrayal, rejection, and disappointment to the character or intent of others. Likewise, we convince ourselves that these feelings are a testament to God not having our best interests at heart.

· · • • • • • · ·

We sometimes interpret other people's views of us as a reflection of God's thoughts. For Jacob, the animosity between himself and his family seemed to reflect his relationship with God. He couldn't help but feel that the tension was a sign of a larger conflict with God. We can relate to Jacob in feeling that the way others treat us is a measure of our worthiness or an indication of our spiritual standing. We think, *if my boss or coworkers don't recognize the worth of my work, God also overlooks it;* or *the external pressure I'm experiencing must be a sign that I'm inadequate in God's eyes, too.*

For older generations, your life was a gauge of the condition of your faith. Your life was thought to mirror the state of your spiritual life. The common saying goes that *if you take care of God's business, He'll take care of yours.* By attending your local church, following your spiritual leader, daily prayer and scripture reading, and serving those in need, you can have confidence that God will bless everything in your life. Despite being an unfair assessment, this measuring stick is still held against the lives of Millennials.

For example, being a Millennial and unsure about whether you'll be living in an apartment or owning a home in five years may lead some to believe that you're spiritually lacking. Our grandparents were homeowners, and we believe that having more faith would help us become homeowners too, but the truth is that it's not a matter of faith. There are cultural and economic barriers, among other forms of barriers, that are beyond our control. Moreover, it is a question of identity, because we have convinced ourselves that we *are* what we *have*, and that our life's meaning is determined by the milestones we reach.

The enduring nature of the covenant in Jacob's wrestling is a crucial point to emphasize for our generation before this chapter ends. Jacob's covenant status remained unchanged throughout the wrestling match, regardless of whether he emerged victorious or not. This serves as encouragement for us that even in wrestling, we are still in covenant. It reassures us that our willingness to wrestle is not a hindrance to God's plan, but a necessary part of it.

His grace extends even when you're uncertain of what lies ahead. You can ask questions without worrying about being disqualified. Even if you make a misstep, it doesn't mean you're out of the game. Labels do not disqualify you. Our questions, missteps, and labels matter to God more than our post-therapy selves, resumes, or curated lives. Even in our darkest moments of struggle, we can trust in God's unwavering presence. When we are weak, He stands with us.

THE GOD OF THE MILLENNIALS

By examining the areas where Millennials struggle, we can gain insight into how God is working in our generation.

Take time to reflect on the areas where you've felt let down, not just by humans, but also by God. While wrestling may seem like an empty pursuit, the quest for a meaningful faith is a struggle that is worth undertaking. Our generation's mission is to persist and endure until we are completely transformed, until we have dismantled our self-serving idols, and until we have eliminated every fault-finding label that has been assigned to us.

Jacob received an impartation from God that proved to be a source of strength for him as he continued on his journey. Our ability to confront and overcome the obstacles of our time will shape our endurance and enable us to accomplish our part of the race before handing over the baton to the next generation.

"When God, your God, ushers you into the land he promised through your ancestors Abraham, Isaac, and Jacob to give you, you're going to walk into large, bustling cities you didn't build, well-furnished houses you didn't buy, come upon wells you didn't dig, vineyards and olive orchards you didn't plant. When you take it all in and settle down, pleased and content, make sure you don't forget how you got there—God brought you out of slavery in Egypt. Deeply respect God, your God. Serve and worship him exclusively. Back up your promises with his name only. Don't fool around with other gods, the gods of your neighbors, because God, your God, who is alive among you is a jealous God."

- Deuteronomy 6:10-19 (MSG)

Chapter Seven

BEYOND

E very generation faced natural or spiritual famines. God instructed Abraham to flee from his homeland, promising to reveal a land to him when the time came. Despite his temptation to flee, Isaac remained in Gerar as God had instructed, trusting in His promised provision.

Isaac advised Jacob to escape to his uncle Laban's house and remain there until the situation with Esau calmed down. It wasn't until decades later that God instructed Jacob to flee from Laban, commanding him to return to his homeland. A pattern of fleeing emerged across generations, typically initiated by God's instruction and with His promise of provision.

Today, our response to spiritual famines is fleeing. However, we are fleeing aimlessly without any structure, direction, or source of provision. Even though we don't use wells anymore, we still need a concrete source to maintain structure and standards in our spiritual lives.

Considering the generational faith that has been passed down to us, what steps can we take in the present to apply it? How can a generation focused on self-fulfillment redirect their focus to serve others and honor God through their faith and the Christian mission?

We must move beyond the wells.

BEYOND THE WELLS

John 4 describes Jesus resting at a well near Sychar, a Samaritan city, after walking a long distance from Judea to Galilee. According to tradition, this well located on the field given by Jacob to his son Joseph was known as Jacob's Well.

Jesus saw a Samaritan woman at the well and asked her for a drink. Though she didn't know who he was, the woman recognized the man as a member of the Jewish community. She was curious why he would inquire about receiving a drink from her, considering the longstanding tension between Jews and Samaritans.

Jesus disrupted the pattern by breaking social barriers and speaking to this woman, and then requesting a favor from her. What established pattern in your life is He trying to interrupt?

Jesus knew that the water from the well could not compare to the spiritual nourishment he could provide. In the presence of God, our shortcomings, weaknesses, and insufficiencies are often magnified. His purity makes our own uncleanness painfully obvious. In the warmth of His unconditional love, we feel the coldness of our own hearts.

"Jesus replied, 'If you only knew the gift God has for you and who you are speaking to, you would ask me, and I would give you living water.' 'But sir, you don't have a rope or a bucket,' she said, 'and this well is very deep. Where would you get this living water? And besides, do you think you're greater than our ancestor Jacob, who gave us this well? How can you offer better water than he and his sons and his animals enjoyed?' Jesus replied, 'Anyone who drinks this water will soon become thirsty again. But those who drink the water I give will never be thirsty again. It becomes a fresh, bubbling spring within them, giving them eternal life.'" - John 4:10-14

Although Jacob may have been the one who dug the well, it was never about him or the wells. The wells and faith of the patriarchs were means to the end: Christ. They played a similar role to John the Baptist, who was the forerunner of Christ. The wells were a lifeline, especially during difficult times. However, their sustainability had an expiration date.

We should strive to leave a legacy that points towards Christ, just as Jacob's well pointed towards the living water. It's not about our accomplishments or influence, but about how our lives reflect the character of Christ. This legacy is timeless and will live on forever.

It was only beyond the well that the Samaritan woman could receive what Christ had to offer. The message to the

Jacob generation of today is to heed the warning and take up the challenge of moving beyond the wells.

It's important to value natural heritage, but it's not the only thing that matters in life. We are meant to fulfill a purpose that transcends the boundaries of time. Beyond being sources of water, the wells dug by the patriarchs pointed to a greater promise of eternal life through Christ. It isn't about us, and it never was.

········

In John 7, Christ promises living water again, this time referring to the Holy Spirit who would come after His ascension. The Holy Spirit is the living water that flows within us. Our faith can continue through generations when we trust in Him, even when the structures we once depended on are gone.

The Holy Spirit is not like a personal assistant, whose sole purpose is to move along a person's agenda. He is not a buddy who condones behaviors and mindsets that need to be changed. The Holy Spirit, being God Himself, takes up residence within us, and by doing so, provides us with the will, capacity, wisdom, and strength necessary to fulfill the will of God.

It is impossible to believe in Christ or pass down faith without the Holy Spirit. The Spirit enables us to serve God. He has the power to remind us of everything and teach us everything we need to know in Christ. The Holy Spirit is an irreplaceable source of truth that cannot be substituted by any other means of knowledge, including mediumship, astrology, psychic knowledge, palm readings, or any other ways to know the truth apart from God.

If we seek to live lives of faith, we need the Holy Spirit. We have enough services, programs, launches, and numbers. We are lacking in the Spirit. It is Him we need.

THINKING GENERATIONALLY

Moving beyond the wells is a challenge that can only be met by adopting a new way of thinking, which I call "generational thinking."

When we adopt a mindset that considers the long-term effects of our actions, we begin to understand that the way we live our lives is not just about us, but about the world we will leave behind for future generations. Generational thinking grasps the temporality of our existence and acknowledges that each individual is part of a whole.

Throughout Scripture, there are many examples of enemy nations seeking to obstruct the faith of Israel. During Isaac's lifetime, the Philistines were filling up the wells. But let's not be mistaken. The reason they were stopping the wells wasn't because they wanted the land. The Philistines' gods were in direct opposition to Yahweh, the God of Israel.

Their opposition was recurrent, and this attempt was one of many. David recognized God as the target of opposition in his encounter with Goliath. Even after David's defeat of the giant, the Philistines continued to be a threat to Israel. David's win was a single step on the path to victory for the nation.

While God has a plan that extends across generations, Satan does also. Today, generational faith is still being threatened by satanic attempts. The enemy is defying God by attempting to stop up our wells and obstructing the continuation of generational faith. However, these famines have been faced before, and our enemy is not a stranger.

Just like Millennials, Generation X and the Boomer generation encountered their own spiritual battles and giants that had to be confronted and overcome. The opposition we are facing is not exclusive to us, and though it may not feel like it, we are not alone.

Generational thinkers recognize that they don't face generational attacks alone. They understand that it takes more than one person to break generational curses or defeat generational enemies. They perceive the worth of a collective response to the attacks of the enemy.

INHERITING GOD

Many generations thrived on the wells of the patriarchs, and from their lineage came the twelve tribes of Israel. When the division of the land of Canaan was taking place among the various tribes, the tribe of Levi was not given any portion of the land. Instead, God said to him, "I am your inheritance, your portion" (Num. 18:20; Josh. 13:33).

This inheritance was carried out through the Levitical priesthood. It was their duty to oversee the worship of the entire nation of Israel. By receiving offerings from the people, they could sustain their livelihood and continue their work.

They were granted cities on land belonging to other tribes, but the amount given seemed smaller when compared to what the other tribes received. They had little land for comfort or security, and at first glance, it may seem they were at a disadvantage. But while the other tribes gained land, Levi's tribe gained the greatest inheritance of all—God Himself.

To move beyond the wells, we must not lose sight of the big picture. Had Jacob and Esau considered future generations, might they have reconciled sooner? Esau's primary concern was his own benefit from the covenant, and he was willing to murder his brother for it. What if he had weighed the impact of the covenant, regardless of who the blessing went to?

Generational thinking demands we teach our children to trust in God's sufficiency. And not only proclaim it but live by it. Our accountability lies in exemplifying the principles we teach. We share the same responsibility as the Israelites in teaching future generations to worship and live for God only.

We cannot caution against the creation of self-serving idols while concealing our own. We must put into action the principles we proclaim. If we trust God for our sufficiency, our words and actions should mirror that reliance.

We must make it abundantly clear to our children that choosing God does not in any way diminish or detract from the richness and quality of life that we experience. Contrary to popular belief, faith is not a liability or weakness. It is our greatest asset.

As a generation that wants it all, we must be mindful not to teach our children to find fulfillment and purpose in God *plus*. God is sufficient without any additives or supplements in our lives. He is not just our portion, but our all.

Should we take this to mean that we should not pursue opportunities, dreams, or endeavors? No, it means our affections, our identities, and our values should not be placed in or determined by them.

CHOOSING DIFFERENT

When we move beyond the wells, we are not only creating a better future for ourselves but also for future generations, who will have the opportunity to chart their own course without the pressure of familial expectations. Moving beyond the wells is crucial in helping younger generations escape the burden of having to choose the same paths, careers, and education as older generations. God's covenant is not confined to any single structure, path, or decision.

Even before our birth, we are already part of God's intergenerational plan. This understanding does not diminish our responsibility, but it does make it easier to bear when we know we are not alone. Just because our parents and grandparents took a certain path doesn't mean we have to; we have the chance to embrace our unique journey.

I would like to add that our responsibility as a younger generation goes beyond just doing things differently from the older generation; we must also resist the cultural norms and do things differently than what society suggests. The faith that we are called to follow is not only countercultural but also disruptive to existing systems and patterns. It is not self-seeking, and it requires us to step out of our comfort zones.

In choosing to do things differently, there are three essential questions to consider:

1. How can we build the kingdom?

2. How can we determine God's will and purpose for our individual paths?

3. In what ways is the gospel relevant to the practice of faith in our modern context?

BUILDING THE KINGDOM

Upon their return from Babylon, the Jews acted on King Cyrus' decree and began rebuilding the temple in Jerusalem. The temple's foundation was restored, and the altar was repaired. They were making progress until the Samaritan neighbors came to stir up trouble.

These neighboring enemies attempted to collaborate with the Jews in an effort to undermine their work, but the Jews refused. When their initial efforts failed, they tried to intimidate and discourage them, but the work continued.

They finally resorted to bribing the officials to legally force them to stop building.

After seeing no change for over a decade, the Jews turned their attention to their own homes and livelihoods. What began as a reaction to opposition and adherence to the law, evolved into a sixteen-year-long excuse.

The prophet in the book of Haggai criticized the Jews for neglecting the reconstruction of the temple while building their own homes. They put off the temple work, saying that the timing wasn't right. But they had convinced themselves that it was the right time to build for themselves, though. Haggai rebuked them and warned that unless they focused on rebuilding God's temple, their personal needs would go unfulfilled.

Kingdom living requires us to be more than just focused on ourselves. As we build our names and empires, are we also building up the kingdom? Our current strategies may ensure security of "the bag", but have we taken into account the goals of the kingdom and how our spiritual journeys will affect future generations?

How has the world's frustration, opposition, distraction, and destructive partnerships caused delays in our work to build the kingdom? The enemy would be thrilled to convince Millennials to stop altogether, and we dread a future where legal decrees could hinder Christian worship and ministry completely. Following Haggai's example, I implore us to do whatever is needed to keep progressing the kingdom's work. Kingdom work follows God's agenda, not personal or political agendas.

The reconstruction of the temple wasn't for God, but for the Jews. In biblical times, only certain physical locations like the Ark of the Covenant or the temple in Jerusalem allowed access to God's presence. Deep mourning marked the Jews' time of exile in Babylon, as they believed that being away from their homeland meant being cut off from God.

As they walked through the foreign land, they couldn't help but wonder if God was still with them. It's no surprise that so many individuals in the Bible sought and cherished the assurance of God's presence. Unbeknownst to them, God remained by their side even after the temple was destroyed, during their exile, and when they were too self-absorbed to notice.

The Jews had to move beyond the temple to grasp that its reconstruction was for their benefit, not God's. They had to shift their perspective and recognize the true purpose of the temple.

In the same way, we need to move beyond the wells and focus on the kingdom. Our plans and pursuits must not take priority over God. Our focus should always be on making room for Him before we make room for more wealth, prosperity, or relationships, because it is only through Him that we can truly find fulfillment and joy. He is with us whether or not we welcome His presence. However, He is more interested in dwelling *within* us than just being present *with* us.

If we are to continue in the work of building the kingdom, we must remember that we ourselves are sanctuaries where God resides through the Holy Spirit. Before taking on extra assignments, we need to examine our lives from the inside out and ensure that everything is in order. We are the starting point for the work of the kingdom. Kingdom living is a manifestation of our inner state. How we choose to prioritize the kingdom will determine the success of any other endeavors we pursue in our lifetime.

We should express our gratitude to God for His infinite mercy and grace which He continues to extend towards us even when we are neglectful of the responsibilities that He has entrusted us with. His mercy flows from the fact that He comprehends our limitations and is unwilling to act against His own character. It is impossible for Him to be any less than faithful.

Although we would like to believe that our cooperation is necessary for God to do His part, the truth is that He remains faithful regardless of our actions. His faithfulness never falters, even when we lack faith and have nothing to bring to the table.

Still, God has assigned the furtherance of the gospel and ministry to disciples of Christ. While He is able to fulfill His universal plan without us, He does not desire to. He has chosen us to be active participants. Therefore, if we long to see change, we cannot turn our backs on the Church.

We cannot be inactive and expect change, but we have to be intentional in our approach. Building the kingdom requires the help of many, and without mercy, it cannot be accomplished.

SEEKING THE WILL OF GOD

What is God's will for my life?

Whether we're searching for the perfect job, considering moving to a different city, or contemplating marriage,
this question can be daunting. Every stage of life presents
us with tough choices that can alter our path. We pray for
God's direction and a sense of peace that we are on the right
track.

Building ourselves up spiritually is crucial to the building of the kingdom; we cannot achieve one without the
other. It all comes back to this—looking at our lives from
the inside-out. The kingdom will only be as strong as we are
individually, so we must not neglect our own growth.

Moving beyond the wells requires a willingness to sur-
render the formulaic approach to God's will. If I do *x*, then
God will do *y*. Or if He reveals Himself through *x* or in *y* way,
this other option cannot be in alignment with His will for my
life. We place a lot of importance on confirmation as it helps
us make sound decisions and act on promptings we feel. But
despite the importance of confirmation, if we waited for it
in every instance, we would never make any progress.

God is not just in the wells. He may want to reveal
Himself and show up in your life in a new way, but it could
be beyond the wells. It could be beyond your position in
church, the family business, your spiritual gifts, or whatever
else you have attached God's favor or blessing to. Do not

limit His provision to familiar wells. Open your eyes to the possibilities beyond what you can currently see.

When it comes to discerning God's will for your life, though you may not possess the same power and authority as God, you are still a co-agent, or partner with God. This means you are capable of making your own decisions with free will.

Instead of offering you a six-step program to discern your next move, I challenge you to discover what happens when you move with freedom, knowing that you are under covenant. Take the steps and leave the ordering to God.

THE GOSPEL'S RELEVANCE TODAY

I believe the gospel settles the old school versus new school debate in our local churches. The dilemma of whose way is the right way to "do" church mirrors the early church's conflict surrounding the Law and grace. I want to emphasize that I am comparing, not equating, the Law to legalism and traditional customs that are no longer applicable to our modern church contexts. My comparison is not an equation, but an illustration to aid our discussion.

I am reminded of Paul's exhortation to the Galatians: "Christ has set us free to live a free life. So take your stand! Never again let anyone put a harness of slavery on you" (Gal. 5:1, MSG). When we cling to rules and formulas for grace, we miss out on the true meaning and depth of the freedom Christ died to give us. Paul was conveying the message to them that although circumcision was not inherently bad, it no longer served its original purpose because of the grace and freedom that was attained through Christ. It had lost its relevance in light of Christ.

Following the Law kept the Jews aware of the expectations placed upon them. Likewise, spiritual wells of tradition have served their intended purposes for older generations. Their legalistic approach, although strict, helped them stay mindful of God's standards. The traditional way of "doing" church is not a sin. The challenge arises when we recognize that certain aspects of tradition no longer function in our contemporary world.

Through his letters to the Galatians and the Romans, Paul sought to bridge the gap between the Jews and the Gentiles, emphasizing the importance of acceptance and unity. By discussing sin's corruption of the Law, Christ's fulfillment of it, and the Spirit's sanctification, he illustrated how the Law had external and social implications as well as internal and spiritual implications.

Paul disagreed with the notion that believers could earn favor with or merit from God by following the Law. The purpose of the Law was not for people to perfectly obey it, as God knew they wouldn't be able to. Rather, it was meant to produce a consciousness of sin that would lead to an unwavering dependence on Him and His grace.

Sin's manipulation caused the people to become preoccupied with their inability to keep the Law, rather than relying on God's grace to maintain their covenant. They turned their backs on God as a loving Father and began to view Him as someone who could never be satisfied.

The Law was not intended to condemn, but it was sin that brought about condemnation. The problem was no longer the incapability of humans to adhere to the Law but striving to secure salvation through their own efforts.

The Law's inability to overcome sin made it hopeless, and this was challenging for Old Testament believers to accept. As a result, they lived under the weight of the Law. They saw the Law as the ultimate measure of their worth, and they believed any misstep was because of a lack of effort. Sin had manipulated the very Law that was meant to lead them to God, causing it to become a never-ending cycle of self-reliance and judgment. But God had a plan: He would send His Son.

In Matthew 5:17, Jesus said, "Don't misunderstand why I have come. I did not come to abolish the law of Moses or the writings of the prophets. No, I came to accomplish their purpose." Christ's sacrifice fulfilled the purpose of the Law, which was to establish a relationship between God and humanity. Thanks to Jesus, humanity has been liberated from the curse of the Law, a heavy burden of incapacity and despair that we could not overcome on our own.

The Spirit's work in us as believers enables us to fulfill the Law with sincerity and from our hearts, freeing us from fruitless obligation. As followers of Christ, we are no longer under the Law but instead are led by the Spirit. Therefore, we are no longer held accountable for the condemnation that once resulted from sin's misuse of the Law (Rom. 8:1).

Sin's influence on customs and practices throughout many generations has caused us to adopt a legalistic mindset in our relationship with God. Its manipulation has been so pervasive that no generation has been able to escape its impact. It is the reason we are currently wrestling so much with our faith.

Even though we make an effort to avoid legalism, our spiritual performance remains the yardstick against which we measure our relationship with God. Our approach to measuring God's love for us and satisfaction with our lives involves analyzing the degree to which we have been engaging in "good Christian behavior."

The message that Paul was trying to convey to both the Jews and Gentiles was to not get too carried away with performance, as our humanity automatically disqualifies us from living a perfect life. Christ is not only the foundation of our faith but also the One who perfects it, and it is Him we must look to for guidance.

To prevent sin from using the Law to condemn us through works-righteousness, we should yield to the Spirit to accomplish God's will. The real work lies within, not just in what we do. The Holy Spirit fulfills the Law written on our hearts, so we still have grace even if we can't keep it perfectly. This grace reminds us of why God gave the Law in the first place: relationship.

· · · · · · · · · ·

The Law, according to Paul's understanding, isn't the opposite or lack of grace. Rather than emphasizing "Law versus grace", the emphasis is on viewing the Law through the lens of grace, made possible by Christ's fulfillment.

For us, it is not about attire, worship styles, or who holds the perfect attendance record. It is not a matter of choosing between old school or new school. It is about the gift of grace that has been given by God to every generation.

The lives that our parents and grandparents led may have differed vastly from ours, but their experiences have influenced the way we, as Millennials, interpret and apply our faith.

If we are to truly welcome and embrace multi-generationality within our congregations, it is necessary that we view the generational wells of faith that were passed down to us through a lens of grace.

Furthermore, we must be intentional in creating spaces for everyone's stories to be heard and opportunities for individuals from different generations to serve together.

Paul addressed the "Law versus grace" debate because the Jews, who had been circumcised and who had experience with the Law, began to see themselves as superior to the Gentiles, who appeared to be taking the easy route through the unfamiliar concept of grace.

In our local churches, is important that older generations do not equate eldership with superiority. Being of greater age does not indicate greater importance within the kingdom. Many Christian adults in the Millennial generation are frustrated with feeling overlooked in ministry or being treated as spiritual infants because of their age range.

If older generations do not see younger generations as spiritually mature enough to partner with in ministry work, there will be a lapse when it is time to pass the baton.

This is one explanation for why there are churches in our local communities with Boomer and Gen X congregants worried about how their church will continue after they are gone if Millennials and Gen Z are not joining. A key to intergenerational ministry is equipping and utilizing younger generations *long* before it's time to pass the baton, so that when the time comes, we are not trying to attract and train at the same time.

Additionally, ministry must be a partnered effort among generations. It is not enough to pass the baton and recline to see if or how the next generation pays their dues. As long as we are living, we are responsible for kingdom work. Thus, we must be willing to partner together in the ministry efforts of our local churches, or the gap will never be bridged.

FAITH THAT NEVER RUNS DRY

The Gospel of Matthew opens with an outline of the lineage of Jesus, and I believe it is a beautiful illustration of faith being passed down from one generation to the next. The 42 recorded generations, from Abraham to Jesus, each played a pivotal role in shaping the faith of those who came after them.

Were all generations faithful to God? Absolutely not. Individuals like Jehoram, Ahaz, Amon, and Jeconiah either repeated the sins of their fathers or forged their own paths of wickedness, yet God still used their lives for His purposes. God's plan cannot be derailed by sin or wickedness, no matter how strong they may seem.

Additionally, it is important to note that not all individuals lived grandiose lives. Abihud and Azor, whose names are only mentioned in genealogy records, are believed to have lived simple, unremarkable lives.

In this life, it's inevitable that some of us will make a significant impact that will be remembered for generations to come. Others of us will lead lives that never make headlines, quietly changing the world in our own way. Regardless, every life is valuable and unique. Both the grandiose and the simple are integral to God's plan. Though everyone's journey will differ, the ultimate destination remains the same: Christ.

The inheritance of wells dates back to the very beginning, and new ones are added with each passing generation. Throughout generations, wells of faith have been passed down, each one leaving a lasting impact on how we express our beliefs today. To generate one thing requires the movement of another. Similarly, the continuation of faith is made possible by the movement of previous generations.

Millennials, we cannot give up on faith. We must keep moving. We are not alone on this journey of faith, and we move not in our own strength, but in a unified strength. Our collective strength is what will propel us forward on our journey of faith and remind us we are not alone.

Our faith is not singular, but a legacy of an extensive faith lineage. It is built on the foundation laid by those who came before us.

It is the faith of Abraham to relinquish the familiar and hope against seemingly impossible odds.

It is the faith of Isaac to continue digging, even in the face of loss and betrayal.

It is the faith of Jacob to work diligently and wrestle without shame.

It is the faith of Judah to act with strength, wisdom, and courage.

It is the faith of Tamar to believe that God can bring good out of even the most painful experiences.

It is the faith of Perez to anchor your identity in God, not in the circumstances of life.

It is the faith of Hezron to witness God as the safeguard of your family.

It is the faith of Amminadab to lead the way for the rest of the nation.

It is the faith of Nahshon to courageously lead wanderers through the wilderness.

It is the faith of Salmon to see the marginalized as deserving of love.

It is the faith of Rahab to put differences aside to advance God's plan.

It is the faith of Boaz to sacrifice inheritance to follow a higher calling.

It is the faith of Ruth to turn from cultural idols and worship God only.

It is the faith of Obed to embrace multi-generational wisdom.

It is the faith of Jesse to accept God's will when it conflicts with your own.

It is the faith of King David to experience God's mercy in your imperfection.

It is the faith of Solomon to trust that wisdom is far more valuable than power.

It is the faith of Rehoboam to lead amid division.

It is the faith of Asa to disrupt the family system and write a new narrative.

It is the faith of Jehoshaphat to triumph over a large army of adversaries.

It is the faith of Uzziah to recognize God as the source of prosperity.

It is the faith of Jotham to learn from your parent's mistakes.

It is the faith of Hezekiah to choose God's way when it's not popular.

It is the faith of Manasseh to know that you are never out of reach of God's mercy.

It is the faith of Josiah to initiate religious reforms to counteract the influence of pop culture.

It is the faith of Zerubbabel to return and rebuild after loss.

It is the faith of Eliakim to be promoted at precisely the right time.

It is the faith of Zadok to experience the bountiful harvest of worship.

It is the faith of Joseph to obey God even when it means risking your reputation.

It is the faith of Mary to see the miraculous in the mundane, bringing forth the Messiah, who is the very basis of our faith.

It is the faith of the disciples to leave everything behind to follow Christ.

It is the faith of Christ who, for the hope set before Him, endured the cross.

It is the faith of Paul to see God's goodness in affliction.

It is the faith of the New Testament church to welcome the Holy Spirit and eagerly await Christ's return.

It is the faith of the early church to stay committed to faith in times of persecution.

It is the faith of the Lost Generation to seek God beyond the confines of tradition.

It is the faith of the Greatest Generation to persevere through adversity.

It is the faith of the Silent Generation to believe change is possible if you have the courage to speak up.

It is the faith of the Baby Boomer Generation to know Christ in suffering.

It is the faith of Generation X to find purpose despite being overlooked.

Millennials, what will be said of *our* faith?

No matter how our faith develops, it is well. It is well with the faith we have inherited, and it is well with the faith we will pass down. In questioning, it is well. In wrestling, it is well. In prevailing, it is well. In grief, it is well. In rejoicing, it is well. In times of sowing, it is well. In harvest, it is well. Our faith, in all seasons, is well.

From the early stages of life to the later stages, it is well. With our faith, our souls, our families, our vocations, and our relationships, it is well. The future is uncertain, and we can't help but wonder what kind of world our children, grandchildren, and great-grandchildren will grow up in. But rest assured, it is well.

May we all, like those praised for their faith in Hebrews, look ahead to a far greater home beyond this earth. Our work here is meaningful, but it's just a piece of the bigger picture. The responsibility lies in our hands to ensure that faith doesn't dry up with us. So, let's move like the faith of the next generations depends on it, because it does.

Through faith, it will be well, and through faith, it *is* well.

"And Lord, haste the day
when my faith shall be sight
The clouds be rolled back as a scroll
The trump shall resound,
and the Lord shall descend
Even so, it is well with my soul."

Lyrics by Horacio Spafford & Phillip Bliss

Dear Reader,

Thank you for dedicating some of your reading time to *It is Well*. If you enjoyed this book, please share a review wherever you get your books, and spread the word to your friends, family, and local community.

Notes

Chapter Two: Boomers

[1] Ryback, M. D., Ralph. (2016, February 22). From Baby Boomers to Generation Z: A detailed look at the characteristics of each generation. *Psychology Today.* Used with permission of Ralph Ryback, M. D.

[2] Taken from The Pursuit of God by A. W. Tozer. Copyright © 2013. Used by permission of Baker Publishing Group.

[3] Taken from Celebration of Discipline: Path to Spiritual Growth by Richard J. Foster. Copyright © 1978, 1988, 1998 by Richard J. Foster. Used by permission of HarperCollins Christian Publishing. www.harpercollinschristian.com

[4] "The Factors Driving the Growth of Religious 'Nones' in the U.S." Pew Research Center, Washington, D.C. (2016) https://www.pewresearch.org/short-reads/2016/09/14/the-factors-driving-the-growth-of-religious-nones-in-the-u-s/.

[5] Taken from Renovation of the Heart: Putting on the Character of Christ by Dallas Willard (Colorado Springs, CO: NavPress, 2002)

[6] Taken from The Pursuit of God by A. W. Tozer. Copyright © 2013. Used by permission of Baker Publishing Group.

[7] Taken from The Pursuit of God by A. W. Tozer. Copyright © 2013. Used by permission of Baker Publishing Group.

[8] E. M. Bounds, *"E. M. Bounds on Prayer"* (New Kensington, PA: Whitaker House, 2012), 119. Used by permission of Whitaker House.

[9] Alison Aughinbaugh, Omar Robles, and Hugette Sun, "Marriage and divorce: patterns by gender, race, and educational attainment," Monthly Labor Review, U.S. Bureau of Labor Statistics, October 2013, https://doi.org/10.21916/mlr.2013.32

[10] Taken from Divine Conspiracy: Rediscovering Our Hidden Life in God by Dallas Willard. Copyright © 2018 by Dallas Willard. Used by permission of HarperCollins Publishers.

[11] Used with permission of InterVarsity Press, from Hearing God: Developing a Conversation with God, Dallas Willard, 2021; permission conveyed through Copyright Clearance Center, Inc.

[12] "A Brief Overview of Black Religious History in the U.S." Pew Research Center, Washington, D.C. (2021) https://www.pewresearch.org/religion/2021/02/16/a-brief-overview-of-black-religious-history-in-the-u-s/.

13 Douglass, Frederick. 1855. "My Bondage and My Freedom".

14 Baldwin, James. *The Fire Next Time.*

Chapter Three: Isaac

15 Taken from Ordering Your Private World by Gordon MacDonald. Copyright © 1984, 1985, 2003 by Gordon MacDonald. Used by permission of HarperCollins Christian Publishing. www.harpercollinschristian.com

16 Taken from Ordering Your Private World by Gordon MacDonald. Copyright © 1984, 1985, 2003 by Gordon MacDonald. Used by permission of HarperCollins Christian Publishing. www.harpercollinschristian.com

17 Taken from Ordering Your Private World by Gordon MacDonald. Copyright © 1984, 1985, 2003 by Gordon MacDonald. Used by permission of HarperCollins Christian Publishing. www.harpercollinschristian.com

Chapter Four: Gen X

18 Kate Bowler, Everything Happens for a Reason (New York: Random House, 2018) Used by permission of Penguin Random House LLC (US).

19 "The Factors Driving the Growth of Religious 'Nones' in the U.S." Pew Research Center, Washington, D.C. (2016).

Acknowledgements

To the author and perfector of our faith. None of this would be possible without You.

To my husband and best friend, André. It seems like just yesterday this book was only an idea. From being a sounding board for the 'aha' moments and late-night brain dumps to making sure I could step away without mom guilt to write when needed, you've been there, and I can't thank you enough.

To my children. You aren't yet old enough to read, but you were in my arms and by my side throughout 99% of this writing process, and I wouldn't have had it any other way. You were constant reminders of why the message of this book is so important.

To my great-uncle, my Uncle Ronnie. The depth of your wells has been evident to me from as early as I can remember. You've never been one for fanfare, but I've always been your biggest fan. My gratitude for you is eternal.

To Dr. Chandler, Dr. Solomon, Dr. Gossmann, Adrianna, Kashina, Jordan, and Kyle for the generous and heartfelt endorsements. I will forever be grateful.

To Ashley for embodying the message of *It is Well* in a way only you can. You are a gift to the world, and I appreciate you lending your artistry to this work.

To my village for your friendship, support, and prayers in all seasons. You all know who you are.

To the readers of *It is Well* for embarking on this journey with me to explore intergenerational faith. I pray it has left a lasting imprint on your hearts as your readership has on mine.

ABOUT THE AUTHOR

Kayleon Dortch-Elliott lives in North Carolina with her husband and children. She is the author of *It is Well* and CEO of Write on the Margin Publishing, LLC. Her mission is to meet Christians in the margins of faith and everyday life. Through her words, she strives to underline a faith that was never meant to be abstract. To learn more about Kayleon and sign up for the *Notes in the Margin* Newsletter, visit www.kayleondortchelliott.com.

NOTES IN THE MARGIN

A BI-WEEKLY NEWSLETTER
FROM AUTHOR KAYLEON DORTCH-ELLIOTT

More than a newsletter. It's a community.

Whether on pages of a book or looseleaf paper, school assignments or office memos, notes in the margin are common. They personalize the reading experience, giving the reader a break from the perfectly formatted body of text to engage and consider portions of the text that are most important to them. Margins offer space for commentary, thoughts, questions, feedback, 'aha' moments, and more.

When it comes to faith, there is ample space in the margins. May the *Notes in the Margin* bi-weekly newsletter, along with Kayleon's published works, inspire you to pause and reflect in the margins of life and faith. To take time to reflect, ponder, ask, and engage. So your faith will extend beyond theory to an applied faith. Because faith was never meant to be abstract.

Sign up for *Notes in the Margin at*
www.kayleondortchelliott.com